For UK order enquiries: please contact Bookpoint Ltd,
130 Milton Park, Abingdon, Oxon OX14 4SB.
Telephone: +44 (0) 1235 827720. *Fax*: +44 (0) 1235 400454.
Lines are open 09.00–17.00, Monday to Saturday, with a 24-hour
message answering service. Details about our titles and how to
order are available at www.hoddereducation.com

British Library Cataloguing in Publication Data: a catalogue record
for this title is available from the British Library.

Copyright © 2011 Clive Erricker

Typeset by MPS Limited, a Macmillan Company.

Printed in Great Britain for Hodder Education, an Hachette UK Company,
338 Euston Road, London NW1 3BH, by CPI Antony Rowe,
Berkshire RG1 8EX

The publisher has used its best endeavours to ensure that the URLs
for external websites referred to in this book are correct and active
at the time of going to press. However, the publisher and the
author have no responsibility for the websites and can make no
guarantee that a site will remain live or that the content will remain
relevant, decent or appropriate.

Hachette UK's policy is to use papers that are natural, renewable
and recyclable products and made from wood grown in sustainable
forests. The logging and manufacturing processes are expected to
conform to the environmental regulations of the country of origin.

Impression number   10 9 8 7 6 5 4 3 2 1
Year   2015 2014 2013 2012 2011

London Borough of Enfield		
91200000049860		
Askews & Holts	May-2011	
294.3	£5.99	

Note on terminology

Due to the difference in languages used by the Theravadin and
Mahayanist branches of Buddhism (Pali and Sanskrit respectively),
Buddhist terms can appear in two forms: for example, *dhamma* (Pali)
and *dharma* (Sanskrit). The Buddha's name also varies accordingly:
Siddhatta Gotama (Pali) and *Siddhartha Gautama* (Sanskrit).
The glossary indicates the alternative renditions of terms used in
this book.

Contents

The Triratna Buddhist Order

In April 2010 the Western Buddhist Order became known as the Triratna Buddhist Order. In the same way, the Friends of the Western Buddhist Order (FWBO) are now known as the Triratna Buddhist Community. This new name reflects the organisation's increasingly global focus in offering refuge to the three jewels – Buddha, Dharma, Sangha. The sanskrit term 'triratna' translates as 'three jewels'. Wherever possible, *Buddhism Made Simple* uses this new terminology. However, publications previously ascribed to the FWBO are still credited as such, and quotations from Order members may also use the previous names.

1

Buddhists and Buddhism

This chapter introduces Buddhism and explains what is distinctive about a Buddhist way of life. It focuses on the importance of the Buddha and his teachings but also on Buddhist practices and the impact they can have on the development of our human faculties, especially the training of the mind. It explains why the idea of community is so important to Buddhists and how that has developed in a distinctive way, involving both lay and monastic members. You will learn about the distinctive features of Buddhist life including the ideal of renunciation, the aspiration to wisdom and compassion and how Buddhists commit themselves to improving themselves and the world they live in. The chapter explains the importance of the precepts as the principles on which a Buddhist way of life is based and mindfulness as the practice that develops the qualities at the heart of the Buddha' teaching.

Who are Buddhists?

Thus shall ye think of all this fleeting world;
A star at dawn, a bubble in a stream;
A flash of lightning in a summer cloud;
A flickering lamp, a phantom, and a dream.

(The Diamond Sutra, 868 AD)

This is a question that many people in the West might well ask. The quotation above is from the Buddha himself, and one answer to our question is that Buddhists are those who understand the world in this way. But such a statement is easily misunderstood, so perhaps we should start by approaching our question in a less poetic fashion.

How would Buddhists today answer it? Some might reply that Buddhists are the followers of the Buddha and his teachings.

While this is an accurate response, it is open to misunderstanding. For example, Buddhists do not follow the Buddha in the same way as Christians follow Christ. The reason for this is that the Buddha is not understood to be a god; nor did he teach his disciples a way to God. Indeed, he did not even claim that his teachings were a unique and original source of wisdom; but he did maintain that they had a very specific practical purpose and that they were meant to be useful.

Buddha always said, 'Don't take what I'm saying, just try to analyse as far as possible and see whether what I'm saying makes sense or not. If it doesn't make sense, discard it. If it does make sense, then pick it up.'

(John Bowker, *Worlds of Faith*, BBC, 1983, p 134)

Another way of answering the question might be to say that Buddhists practise the *dhamma* (Pali) or *dharma* (Sanskrit). This word has a range of meanings that interconnect. Most importantly, dharma means truth, law or teaching. Thus, Buddhists are stressing that the Buddha's teaching pointed to the truth; and moreover, that they are practising what the Buddha preached, truthful living, which is open to everyone.

*The Dhamma can be practised by anybody. It can be practised
by any man, woman, even by any child. It can be practised
by someone in India, and it can be practised by someone in
England. By someone in America, or someone in China. If there
are people on the moon, it can be practised by those people on
the moon. The Dhamma is universal ... it's for everybody – for
every human being. Because every human being is the brother
or sister of every other human being. The more we practise
the Dhamma, the more we come together. It doesn't matter
whether we are born in India or whether we are born in England.
If we practise the Dhamma, we are one. If we practise the
Dhamma, we are brothers and sisters.*

(Ven. Sangharakshita, *Friends of the Western Buddhist Order
Newsletter* No. 54, p 2)

A third answer to the question would be to say that Buddhists
are those who belong to the sangha. Sangha means community.
Often it denotes the monastic community, but in a broader sense
it refers to Buddhists in general. It could be said that Buddhists are
part of the sangha in the way that Christians belong to the Church.
However, the distinction of belonging to the Buddhist community is a
commitment to living a life that cultivates well-being and happiness
through following particular teachings, rules and practices. Sometimes
the members of the sangha are referred to as 'spiritual friends'.

If we put all three answers together, we arrive at a more
complete understanding of what it means to be a Buddhist.

The Three Jewels

The Buddha, dhamma or dharma and sangha are known as
the Three Jewels, the implication of this being that they are what
Buddhists hold most dear in life. It is usual to make a commitment
to them; this takes place in a formal ceremony, which marks the
intention to live a life that can be summarized in a verse found in
the *Dhammapada*, a popular compilation of the Buddha's teaching:

*Not to do evil
To cultivate good
To purify one's mind.*

The importance of this commitment is made clearer by contrasting these Three Jewels with what Buddhists understand to be the unhelpful influences in life, also termed the three poisons: greed or craving, which is sometimes also termed desire; hatred or aversion; and delusion or ignorance. The opposition of these triple formulations succinctly defines the Buddhist path. By inclining to the former, and seeking to avoid the influence of the latter, Buddhists understand the purpose of life.

The Three Refuges

The Buddha, dhamma (dharma) and sangha are also known as the Three Refuges. Refuge is not used in its negative sense of hiding away from something; rather, it means that which provides safety and the possibility of growth, that which you can put your trust in. For this reason, the formal recitation of the Three Jewels is described as 'going for refuge'. Although Buddhists of different persuasions would want to say a lot more about what this means and involves, we may begin here by saying that a Buddhist is one who has taken refuge in the Buddha, dhamma and sangha; from here, like the Buddha himself when he resolved to leave home in search of wisdom, he or she 'goes forth'.

Through the simple act of reciting this formula three times, one declares oneself a Buddhist:

I go for refuge to the Buddha
I go for refuge to the Dhamma
I go for refuge to the Sangha.

Buddhist practice

The Five Precepts (Panca Sila)

At the heart of Buddhist ethical practice are the Five Precepts. These are rules that identify the aspirations of a Buddhist. They are not commandments; rather, they are the minimum essential 'prescription' for treating the human condition, and an antidote to the three poisons: greed, aversion or hatred, and ignorance or delusion. They consist of the following undertakings:

1 *I undertake to observe the precept to abstain from harming living beings.*
2 *I undertake to observe the precept to abstain from taking things not freely given.*
3 *I undertake to observe the precept to abstain from sexual misconduct.*
4 *I undertake to observe the precept to abstain from false speech.*
5 *I undertake to observe the precept to abstain from intoxicating drinks and drugs causing heedlessness.*

(adapted from Niyamatolika, *The Word of the Buddha*,
The Buddhist Publication Society, 1971, p xii)

The Ten Precepts (*Dasa Sila*) and the Eight Precepts (*Attanga Sila*)

The Buddha laid down the Ten Precepts for *samaneras* (those in training for the monastic life) and pious lay people unattached to families. They are the basis of the monastic code followed by *bhikkhus* (monks). The following are added to the basic Five Precepts:

6 *I undertake to observe the precept to abstain from taking untimely meals.*
7 *I undertake to abstain from dancing, music, singing and watching grotesque mime.*
8 *I undertake to abstain from the use of garlands, perfumes and personal adornment.*
9 *I undertake to abstain from the use of high seats.*
10 *I undertake to abstain from accepting gold or silver.*

(The Eight Precepts put numbers seven and eight together and omit the tenth.)

Lay Buddhists may undertake the Eight Precepts on festival days, but the Ten Precepts effectively determine the separation of monks from the rest of society as those who have taken up the mendicant life (relying on others for their physical and material needs), and become renunciants. The ideal behind the practice of the Ten Precepts is to be freed from all sensual entanglements. Thus the prohibitions involved prevent indulgence in food, entertainment, adornment, the seeking of status, personal importance and luxury, and the accumulation of wealth.

In order to emphasize their value, a positive formulation of the precepts is sometimes used, which is recited as follows:

> *With deeds of loving kindness, I purify my body.*
> *With open-handed generosity, I purify my body.*
> *With stillness, simplicity and contentment, I purify my body.*
> *With truthful communication, I purify my speech.*
> *With mindfulness, clear and radiant, I purify my mind.*

(The *FWBO Puja Book*, Windhorse Publications, 1984, p 18)

Mindfulness

The Buddha's teaching stressed as a supreme quality the cultivation of mindfulness; this involves an ability to watch over our own state of mind at the same time as observing the emotional fluctuations that occur in those around us. We cannot give to others without taking account of, and dealing with, the volatility present in our own nature. In simple terms, anger provokes anger, meanness provokes meanness, heedlessness provokes heedlessness. A crucial implication of the Buddha's teaching is that no one is an island, but that by practising the dhamma it is possible to influence the attitudes of those around us and of society at large. Indeed, the substance of this message goes still further. Not only human existence, but the destiny of the world, depend upon this taking place. It involves being in harmony with nature, and respect for all living things. Returning to the Indian context in which this teaching was first formulated, it goes beyond the span of our lives from birth to death, and determines our future rebirth. Buddhists consider that the capacity to progress to a more elevated spiritual and moral state has a fundamental effect on the evolution of the world. Adhering to the dhamma will make the world a more harmonious place; the opposite will be true if the dhamma is ignored. Equally, the individual will find the dhamma easier or harder to follow as a consequence. Thus the microcosmic and macrocosmic understanding of individual action and cosmic evolution are intimately related. The capacity to be virtuous and to exhibit such qualities as generosity and loving kindness are steps on the path to becoming truly compassionate, which is one of the two supreme Buddhist attributes. The Buddha expressed this in one of his sermons to his first disciples:

> ***Go forth on your journey, for the profit of the many, out of compassion for the world, for the welfare, the profit, the bliss of devas (gods) and mankind.***
>
> (*Vinaya* 1:21, quoted in F.L. Woodward, *Some Sayings of the Buddha*, The Buddhist Society, London, 1974)

Wisdom and compassion

Compassion (*karuna*) must be complemented by wisdom (*prajna*). The two are inseparable; they co-exist, and without the other neither is possible. The development of wisdom depends upon a more formal practice which, in Western terms, is understood as meditation. In its earlier Indian context, it was a form of yoga. Yoga means to yoke or bind oneself, and here the notion of commitment is present once again. Without the discipline of a formal practice that allows understanding of the way in which one's own mind works, and development of the capacity for insight, the cultivation of compassion is inevitably diminished. One word for meditation that identifies its instrumental role is *bhavana* (mental or spiritual development); bhavana presumes that the latent capacity we have needs to be cultivated, in order for our full potential to be achieved.

Skilfulness

We have noted that following the precepts, and developing insight through meditation, are two basic and interconnected practices of the Buddhist life, and that through these Buddhists seek to become wiser and more compassionate. There is a third element that plays a necessary part in this development.

Skilfulness, or skill in means (*upaya*), was a supreme quality of the Buddha. As a teacher he was not giving information which, once received, could immediately be understood. In fact, one of the most crucial moments in the Buddha's life came when, after achieving enlightenment (*bhodi*) or awakening, he was daunted by the prospect of trying to convey what he now knew to anyone. He perceived that humans were too caught up in worldly attachments to hear and understand that happiness lay beyond worldly concerns, and that suffering was a result of living in ignorance of this knowledge. His resolve changed, and his teaching career began only when, in the mythological but highly poetic way in which this event is conveyed in the Buddhist scriptures, the god Brahma came to the Buddha and exhorted him, out of compassion for the world, to share his wisdom because, 'There are beings with a little dust in their eyes who, not hearing the Dharma, are decaying.'

For Buddhists, this event, along with the Buddha's first sermon in the Deer Park at Sarnath near Benares, is of seminal importance. This is the point at which the Buddhist tradition began, with the Buddha's resolve to teach the dhamma, and it illustrates why Buddhists often refer to themselves as 'followers of the dhamma' rather than as Buddhists or followers of the Buddha.

Only because the Buddha taught it did the dhamma appear in the world, and only because of the Buddha's supreme skilfulness in the way he taught – by word and deed – was it possible for others to understand and follow the dhamma themselves. This skilfulness is therefore also a quality to which Buddhists aspire, and which they value highly. Without it, the dhamma would not be passed on.

Awakening

The Buddha's great achievement was to attain enlightenment or *nirvana* (*nibbana*). He is said to have attained nirvana under a pipal tree in Bodh-Gaya, in north-east India. In Buddhist tradition, this tree is now named after his achievement and called a *Bodhi* (enlightenment) tree. This event provides the inspiration for all Buddhists. The term 'awakening' perhaps explains the significance of this event in a more accessible way. It is an awakening to the way things truly are, and an extinguishing of the ignorance that fetters us to continual rebirth in the realm of *samsara*, which we can translate as motivation by desire, ignorance and aversion. Nirvana literally means 'to extinguish'.

Nirvana is not a place, in geographical terms, other than where we are. It is not a heaven, in the other-worldly sense of the term. But it is a recognition that our potential is not fulfilled by our day-to-day concern for advancement or survival, nor is it denied by our ultimate fear of extinction or death. The Buddha's teaching is, as one Zen saying puts it, like a finger pointing at the moon. To mistake the teaching for the truth is to misunderstand the nature of the journey.

In conclusion

This chapter has provided a survey of the basic tenets of Buddhism and what constitutes being a Buddhist. Necessarily it has not introduced varieties of interpretations of these tenets, which will emerge in later chapters.

2

the life of the Buddha

This chapter focuses on the Buddha's life and how what he achieved provided the foundation for the Buddhist tradition. It introduces his early experiences and his determination to renounce worldly ambition. It traces his career as a renunciant, one of many in India at that time, and how he created his own path which led to what Buddhists call his awakening, or enlightenment. From that point he became the Buddha, one who has overcome ignorance and suffering, and started his mission. You will learn how his distinctive teachings led to the founding of a monastic community and a lay following based on the rules and practices that he established. This chapter also introduces the distinctive Buddhist goal of nirvana and how the Buddha attained it as a result of his enlightenment, thus overcoming the effects of karma and the necessity of rebirth.

The Buddha's significance

The word 'Buddha' is a title given by his followers to the teacher Siddhartha Gautama (Siddhatta Gotama), who lived in India 2,500 years ago. We might well ask what relevance such a figure and his life can have for us today. Our pursuit of progress in the modern world suggests that we constantly gain more knowledge as time goes by. Yet we only have to reflect on the weight of human suffering that remains and re-emerges throughout human history (and was just as prevalent, if not more so, in the twentieth century) to realize there are certain problems that our accumulated knowledge simply cannot address. More sophisticated technology and scientific advances do not get to the root of the problem of human conflict and suffering. More efficient communication in a technological sense is not to be equated with better communication between human beings. Ultimately, some problems just will not go away, however hard we address them. Such problems can be understood as matters of the heart as well as of the mind.

The Four Sights

Siddhartha was born into comparative privilege, the son of a chief (king or raja) of the Sakya people of north-eastern India (in present-day Nepal). His early life equipped him for government and the inheritance of his father's position. However, his education and social standing also allowed him a degree of choice as to his future; and, so the narrative tells, his father was well aware of this possibility. The traditional story describes how Queen Mahamaya, the wife of King Suddhodama and Siddhartha's mother, was troubled by a dream that was interpreted to mean that she was to have a son who would one day become either a king or a *sadhu* (a holy man who has renounced worldly things). When Siddhartha was born, and throughout his childhood and adolescence, the king was anxious that he should choose the former vocation, and so organized his life to ensure, as far as possible, that this would occur. He was surrounded by beautiful things and kept within the palace grounds. He was married to the beautiful Princess Yasodhara, who then gave birth to their son. The combination of a pleasant, fulfilling life, with the responsibility of a family, was thought to prepare the young prince for his inheritance – socially and psychologically – and his education also reflected this. The king's hope was shattered by what, in Buddhist tradition, is called the Four Sights. Siddhartha grew restless of his palace life, and sought to know of the world outside. He directed his charioteer to take him out into the world beyond the confines of the palace, and encountered experiences that had an abiding effect and shaped his future life. The first time he ventured beyond the palace precincts he saw an old man, and questioned his companion as to why he was so bent and frail. Siddhartha was struck by the answer he was given: that this was the eventual lot of all human beings, including himself. It was a natural and unavoidable event. His response was, 'What is the use of this youth, vitality and strength, if it all ends in this?'

The second sight, on his next excursion beyond the palace, was of a sick person. Again, he was struck by the fact that dis-ease and malady afflict even the strongest and healthiest of individuals and, more importantly, that there is no way of anyone preventing it.

The third sight was of a corpse being carried to the cremation ground on a stretcher. This was, and still is, a common sight in India, where the dead are not hidden from the public eye by coffins or hearses, and where the burning of the dead is open to public view, most conspicuously on the *ghats* beside rivers, for example at Varanasi beside the Ganges. Again, what the charioteer understood to be an everyday event and a typical aspect of life stunned Siddhartha. What struck him most forcibly was the lack of control and direction people ultimately have over their own life and destiny. You don't want to grow old but you can't help it. You don't want to fall sick but you can't ensure against it. Death is unavoidable and yet it makes a nonsense of living. Where is the meaning and purpose in all this? The agonized questioning of Siddhartha is contrasted, in the story, with the unquestioning acceptance of this state of affairs betrayed by Khanna, his charioteer. Siddhartha awoke to the true nature of being in this world, to the state of samsara, characterized by old age, sickness, death and continual becoming. It was pointless nonsense to live with the acceptance that there is nothing humans can do to alter this state of affairs, whatever other knowledge and sophistication they may achieve. For him, perhaps the most striking discovery of these ventures into the outside world was that humans accept this as their lot, as natural.

Siddhartha's reaction to the first three sights exemplifies the Buddhist starting point: seeing to the heart of the matter.

What happens after that, in terms of the decisions one makes and the life one leads, is rooted in the understanding that this is the fundamental problem that must be addressed. Similarly, therefore, we can appreciate that to see that life is characterized by suffering, but not to act upon that awareness, is a wholly 'un-Buddhist' attitude. Such pessimism, or fatalism, is completely contrary to Buddhist understanding. Once the problem has been identified, one is immediately committed to doing something about it. The retrospective telling of the Buddha's journey to enlightenment reveals that, behind the serene smile and composed form of later Buddha images, lies a story of inner struggle revealed in the narratives of the Buddha's life. The story of the Four Sights indicates the resolve of a restless heart to pursue resolutely an uncompromised goal. What is told as four brief excursions into a matter-of-fact and everyday world highlights the significance, for Buddhists, of waking up to the reality that the world we take as given and ordinary is really a fantastic state of affairs. It is only by dwelling on this, and by resolving to transform our own understanding of what it means to take full advantage of a human life, that we can fulfil our human potential.

For Siddhartha, the fourth sight was the inspiration to this end. This fourth sight was of a sadhu, or holy man, walking the streets with his alms bowl. This is a relatively common sight in Indian life. It was, and is, the alternative way of life to that of the householder, the one who has fulfilled his duty of bringing up a family and following a traditional occupation. The sadhu was understood as a mendicant, one who has given up wealth and material gain by virtue of relying on others for his basic sustenance, shelter and livelihood. In contrast to the householder, the sadhu is a 'wandering one' (*anagarika*) who has acknowledged that this ordinary world of change and suffering (called the realm of samsara) is one in which no home, in the spiritual sense, can be found. To put it bluntly, the riddle of existence and human destiny cannot be resolved simply by pursuing one's social duties.

This was the dilemma that confronted Siddhartha. To pursue the life of the sadhu, everything had to be given up: his expected future career, his marriage and family, his security in the life of the palace and his fulfilment of parental expectations. We have no knowledge of how he came to resolve this dilemma, but he did; without that Buddhism would not have come into being.

Going forth

The stories tell how, on the night of a full moon, Siddhartha bade farewell to his sleeping wife and child. He rode to the edge of the Sakya kingdom, divested himself of his clothes, long hair and beard, and resolved to go forth as a wandering one. This event is understood in Buddhist terms as Siddhartha's 'going forth': the moment of commitment to a renunciant's life and the beginning of his search, his new career.

After leaving home, he was confronted with the alternatives available to him in Indian society. Foremost among these were the ascetic practices of yogis who, through austerity and denial of physical nourishment, sought to realize their spiritual aspirations. Subjugation of the flesh was for them a necessary prerequisite to spiritual advancement. (This is not just a matter of historical interest as, in India at least, it is still practised.) Unlike in the West, where the notion of austerity belongs more to the past, as redundant as the monastic life, in India the large number of sadhus who devote themselves to this cause can be witnessed readily at dawn on the banks of the Ganges, and at the great pilgrimage festivals, such as Kumbh Mela in Allahabad, which they attend.

Self-mortification

Siddhartha pursued the path of self-mortification for six years, limiting his food and sleep, not washing and living naked, or in the sky-clad state, as it was known. He gained a reputation among fellow ascetics, gathering disciples and companions. His fame, it is said, spread like the sound of a great gong in the canopy of the sky. Though he achieved states of higher consciousness and greater awareness, he finally gave up these practices because he came to the conclusion that they did not lead to the realization of the truth (the cessation of suffering). He started eating again, and his followers and companions deserted him. He continued to travel alone, seeking out other teachers, but finally became disillusioned by all their practices. He eventually reached a spot where he resolved to remain until he achieved enlightenment. This is now a well-known moment, both in Buddhist tradition and in world history. Beneath the shade of a great pipal tree, later named after this event as a Bodhi (enlightenment) tree, beside a river, he resolved, 'I will not rise from this spot until I am enlightened. Flesh may wither away, blood may dry up, but until I gain enlightenment I shall not move from this seat.'

The enlightenment

It is not easy to imagine what occurred in the mind of one sitting so motionless. It seems ironic that such a great event – the rediscovery of truth – should outwardly be so uneventful. But it is indicative of the character of Buddhism that it should be so: truth is found in silence and stillness rather than activity. He sat there in a meditative state, gaining greater concentration and control of his mind.

This state of purification was not achieved instantly, but was the result of all the training he had undertaken since leaving home. It involved overcoming the mental hindrances that disrupt and unbalance the mind.

We are told that on the night of the full moon of Wesak (the month of May in the Western calendar), the Buddha fixed his mind on the morning star as it was rising, and the moment of full enlightenment occurred.

Essentially, Siddhartha became the Buddha at this point when he eradicated all ignorance, and saw things for exactly what they were with crystal clarity. If we try to imagine what this could be like, we might think of times when, in trying to understand apparently complex, insoluble problems, we have hit on an instant when answers revealed themselves so obviously that it was as though we had previously missed what was right before our eyes; moments when we have said, 'Of course, how could I have been so blind!' This helps us to understand why the event is referred to as 'The Great Awakening', and why the term 'letting go' is so often used by Buddhists to indicate the nature of such wisdom.

Turning the wheel of the dharma

The difficulty of disclosing this truth to others was something that did not immediately resolve itself for the Buddha. As we have seen, he was initially unsure that it could be comprehended by anyone, but the Buddha's teaching career began with his sermon at Sarnath, where he encountered his former companions and preached the dharma for the first time. The distance from Bodh Gaya, the place of his enlightenment, to Sarnath, is one hundred miles, and we can only speculate on what went through his mind while he made the journey. However, when he met his first audience, they were struck by his overall disposition, which radiated those virtues held in high esteem by Buddhists. The confidence and equanimity with which he encountered them were a prelude to the acceptance of his teaching, and drew to him the community that was to grow up around him.

It was not just what the Buddha had to say, but the confidence he inspired in those whom he addressed, that won over his audience. At first, his five former companions greeted him with scepticism, for he was that same Gotama who had given up the path of ascetic practice. However, struck by his authority, they received him back into their company and subsequently became his followers.

The mission

The Buddha practised the life of an itinerant preacher, roaming across north-eastern India for the remainder of his life, from his enlightenment at the age of 35. Following climatic conditions, the pattern he established was to wander from place to place for nine months of the year, and take shelter during the three-month monsoon period; these three months became established as a time of retreat and remain so for some monastic Buddhist communities today.

Taking one meal a day, whenever he came to a village, he established the practice of standing at the villagers' doors silently with his alms bowl; once he had collected sufficient food, he would retire to a mango grove on the outskirts of a village to eat. After his meal, villagers would gather round to hear him teach. In this way, his following increased, drawn from different strata in the caste-orientated Indian society.

The growth of the sangha

Starting with the five former companions, the Buddha's followers grew into an Order of Monks (the *Bhikkhu Sangha*), which drew in lay people to the mendicant life. As the missionary preaching of the order spread, so lay people 'went for refuge' to the Buddha, without renouncing their status as householders, and the lay community developed. This balance between monastic and lay life in the Sangha was one of the main features of the Buddha's mission during his teaching career, which spanned 40 years. It was the blueprint for harmony and balance in the social order that transformed the movement, from its initial character as a mendicant group, into an influential Indian tradition that, centuries later, was to convert the Emperor Ashoka, who sought to rule the sub-continent according to Buddhist principles.

Women had been ordained as members of the Order, though the Buddha's attitude had been ambiguous; he accepted them with some reluctance and warned monks of the need to be vigilant in their presence. In answer to his disciple Ananda's question, asking how monks should behave in the presence of women, he is recorded as saying, 'No talking' and, 'Keep wide awake'. This may be ascribed to his belief that attachment to women was a major obstacle in the attainment of nirvana; whatever the reason, such sayings should be put in the context of the whole code of monastic discipline (*vinaya*) that the Buddha laid down.

Paranirvana

The Buddha's death, in his old age, was said to be by food poisoning, from having inadvertently eaten unwholesome mushrooms, truffles or pork, which had been offered to him. It is said that he passed away in a state of meditation, reclining on his right side, his head supported by his hand. This posture has been recorded in Buddhist iconography, and is understood as the Buddha's passing into *paranirvana* – nirvana without remainder; a state in which he was no longer subject to rebirth. This occurred in the woodlands outside the town of Kusinara. He appointed no successor and, it seems, he wished the Sangha to remain a relatively non-hierarchical organization.

In conclusion

In this chapter we have focused upon the life of the historical Buddha, Siddhartha Gautama, who became known to his followers as Sakyamuni (the sage of the Sakyas) upon achieving liberation. While all Buddhists acknowledge the enlightenment of the historical Buddha, what Buddhahood entailed is interpreted differently in the diverse branches of Buddhism.

3

the Buddha's teaching

This chapter outlines the Buddha's teaching and, in particular, the four Noble Truths and the Eightfold Path. It explains the importance of the Buddha's concept of dukkha (usually translated as dis-ease, unsatisfactoriness or suffering) and why the Buddha's teaching focuses on this and how it can be overcome. The chapter links the foundational teachings to the practices required to make spiritual progress. It also reveals the radical changes required in our perception of the world, ourselves and the way in which we treat others and the obstacles to be overcome. You will learn how, despite being philosophically profound, the Buddha's teaching was always directed to achieving a practical effect through its application in everything that we do in the everyday world. This is expressed succinctly in the Eightfold Path's requirements of Right Speech, Right Action and Right Livelihood and the need for mental discipline.

Thus have I heard. The Blessed One was once living in the Deer Park at Isipatana (the Resort of Seers) near Varanasi (Benares). There he addressed the group of five bhikkhus.

This is the beginning of what is referred to as the first discourse (*darsana*) of the Buddha, as it appears in the collected writings of the Buddhist canon, the *suttas* (*sutras*). Sutta means thread, and this term is used to express the connected ideas that constitute a discourse of the Buddha. In this case, we are listening to the way in which the Buddha formulated his basic understanding of the human condition, and expounded it to those who first listened, his original companions, who were to become his *bhikkhus* (monks or followers).

This teaching addresses the Four Noble Truths and the Middle Way – the crux of the Buddha's teaching pared down to the single concept of *dukkha* (suffering or 'unsatisfactoriness'), why it is the fundamental aspect of the human condition, and how it can be overcome. It relates to the Buddha's own life and experiences:

> *Bhikkhus, these two extremes ought not to be practised by one who has gone forth from the household life. What are the two? There is devotion to the indulgence of sense-pleasures, which is low, common, the way of ordinary people, unworthy and unprofitable; and there is devotion to self-mortification, which is painful, unworthy and unprofitable.*

(W. Rahula, *What the Buddha Taught*, Gordon Fraser, 1982, p 92)

The Buddha knew about indulgence in sensual pleasures from his life in the palace, and about self-mortification from his early renunciant experiences; and by reflecting on these he developed the teaching of the Middle Way, which leads to 'vision, knowledge, calm, insight, enlightenment, Nibbana'.

The Middle Way is also the fourth of the Noble Truths that the Buddha expounded. To understand this, we must first look at the three propositions that lead up to it, which resulted in his exposition of the Buddhist path, and which, together with the fourth, the Middle Way, constitute the Four Noble Truths:

1 *Dukkha*, dis-ease or suffering
2 *Samudaya*, the arising or origin of dukkha

3 *Nirodha*, the cessation of dukkha
4 *Magga*, the way leading to the cessation of dukkha.

The first Noble Truth: all is suffering (dukkha)

It is very difficult to translate the term 'dukkha' accurately. One word, such as suffering, is insufficient and misleading. It is not a purely philosophical term, and it would be wrong to treat it in that way. Suffering is one meaning ascribed to it, but this suggests a pessimistic view, somehow stressing the bad things and ignoring the good that happens in the course of human experience. It is necessary to understand that *experience* is the key word here. What the Buddha is pointing to is the weight of understanding brought about by reflecting on the totality of a life lived, not simply by weighing its pros and cons. Other words that help to elucidate its meaning are dis-ease, imperfection and inadequacy. It is not that life does not have its happy moments as well as the unhappy ones, but that the sum total of human experience is inadequate or imperfect. It is not all one might hope for or expect. Such expectation or hope is not a matter of false optimism or fantasy, rather it is a recognition that what is achieved in life is ultimately insubstantial, fleeting and unfulfilling. The term, *sukkha*, the opposite of dukkha, denotes happiness, comfort and ease. The Buddha's insight is only fully understood by looking at the first three Noble Truths together as a complete analysis of the human situation; but it is already clear from analysing the first Noble Truth that what we wish to achieve lies beyond our reach; not that the goal we seek at any moment is inaccessible, but that the achievement of this goal does not confer the happiness we sought through it. Professional ambition, fame, material wealth, financial security, physical and mental health, romance, admiration and friendship are all understandable goals, but the nature of life is such that we are not fulfilled in our achievements. Whatever we gain in any of these spheres is not enough to satisfy us. Dukkha is a deep-seated internal condition brought about through our relationship with a world that cannot satisfy that which we crave.

However, we cannot fulfil ourselves by changing that world, rather we have to look for a cure for this condition within ourselves. The fundamental reason for this is that the world – in the Buddhist sense of the samsaric realm which we experience – is subject to impermanence. All is impermanent (*anicca*) and subject to change. This is the second aspect of dukkha, in the Buddha's analysis. It is this fact that causes dukkha. We constantly seek to create permanence, to hold on to things, but our aspirations slip through our grasp. This is the important point about the Buddha's description of life being dukkha. Nothing abides: no moment, no feeling, no thought, no person. (This is self-evidently true, at least in the long term, because everybody dies.) However, there are little deaths and new beginnings throughout life – at every moment, in fact. Change is inevitable and necessary; change is the condition of impermanence; impermanence prevents the possibility of anything abiding. This description is neither happy nor sad, optimistic nor pessimistic; from a Buddhist viewpoint, it is a true analysis, the analysis of the one who has an enlightened view and sees clearly.

However, if we bring any sense of sadness or revulsion to this understanding, then this too is understandable from a Buddhist position, because it points to the next proposition.

The second Noble Truth: the origin of suffering (samudaya)

The second Noble Truth recognizes that dukkha goes deeper still, and has even more radical implications.

We are used to thinking about there being *a world I live in* and *I, who live in the world*. In other words, we distinguish quite clearly between ourselves as individuals and the world outside us, which is made up of things, events and people. While this way of understanding ourselves is conventionally and practically useful, it proves dangerous when it becomes rooted too deeply.

Objectively speaking, it would seem highly foolish to suggest that the world – that which is not me – is impermanent, but that *I*, however, *am* permanent. Nevertheless, we often live and think as though that were true. It is as if I am standing alone on a station platform, watching a train go by, and I am aware of the movement of the train; that the people in it are travelling from one place to another; that their lives are changing as they travel along the track between departure and destination; but I am standing still, watching, unmoving, and fully aware of what is happening in front of my eyes.

However, on the train, a person looks out of the window, and as the train passes the station, he sees me standing there alone – in one moment in his present, then just a past image and memory. For me, the passenger moves in time and does not abide; for the passenger I do the same – but the realities perceived are contradictory. In truth, says the Buddha, neither abides. What moves is neither the train nor the person, but the greater, all-embracing, unseen vehicle that passes through train and station alike: time.

Another way of perceiving this view is to imagine standing and staring up at the stars in the night sky, and being aware that what you are seeing is light years away from you and therefore at a considerable distance in *time* from you as well as in *space* (due to the time it takes for the stars' light to reach you). It seems that you are the central fixed point in the universe. Yet now imagine yourself on one of those stars viewing the earth at that same moment. You would not see yourself: you would not yet be there.

Just as Copernicus revolutionized our understanding of the universe, so the Buddha's teaching completely changes the way we understand ourselves. We are also a part of the universe's ceaseless *becoming*; there is no abiding self, but merely a constantly changing and impermanent aspect of that becoming. This Buddhist doctrine of *anatta* (no self) is the third aspect of dukkha; together dukkha, anicca and anatta are known as the three marks, or the fundamental characteristics of being.

The Buddha's teaching emphasizes the fact that life does not have to be like this, moving constantly between desire and aversion; changing states of mind and circumstance within which I identify myself. Desire inevitably leads to aversion, and worldly happiness can never be more than a passing sensation. The only way out of this ceaseless circle is to understand that the 'I' who craves for happiness and contentment is the very obstacle that prevents it. It is born of the ignorance of attachment. Self is dukkha, but letting go of self is true happiness.

Karmic conditioning

The word 'karma' means 'action'. As a result, the relationship between what you do and what happens to you is open to different sorts of explanation. At one end of the scale, it can act as an explanation of why misfortune happens when it is not recognizably the result of particular actions. Common Western explanations of this would be 'luck', 'fate' or 'chance'. In other words, where no obvious historical causal connection can be found, the cause must lie elsewhere. In Indian terms, this would relate back to a previous life and its bad karma, which needs to be worked out in this one. Notice, however, the crucial distinction between the Western and Indian notions. It is not that what happens is inexplicable or random, but that the explanation lies beyond our everyday cognition or observations. Initial reflection may lead to a form of fatalism ('how can I ever know?'), but this is not necessarily the case.

The reason why karma became a central theme in the Buddha's teaching was because he was concerned with liberating individuals from a state of ignorance and suffering.

The importance of karma is that it demonstrates the practicality of Buddhist teachings. Ethical considerations become paramount, because liberating oneself from the dis-ease of samsaric existence is a karmic matter, embedded in our everyday activities and behaviour.

Rebirth

The Buddha's view rooted karma in the process of rebirth, or *re-becoming*. In India, this was a generally recognized idea: that we live through succeeding rebirths that are determined by our karmic habits. When our actions bring about bad effects, we shall reap their consequences in a later life. Equally, good acts will produce a better rebirth. In this way, a rigid distinction between human and other life forms is not made. We may be reborn in a higher or lower human situation, and subject to greater or lesser hardship; but we may also be born in a different form – as an animal, for example, and therefore subject to even greater ignorance.

In the *Jataka Tales* (popular Buddhist fables), the previous rebirths of the Buddha as various animals are recounted: he is reborn as a bird, a monkey, a buffalo and an elephant among others.

It is when the consequences of our ignorance and craving are recognized in this way, and when the state of affairs is understood as endless, that the purchase of the Buddha's teaching is registered more emphatically. The value of a present, relatively comfortable existence is rendered negligible in the light of future striving. Imprisoned in samsara for life sentence after life sentence, it matters little whether your present cell offers comparative ease or luxury, as it cannot last.

If we regard karma and rebirth as speculative theories or ideas, it is unlikely that the Buddha's teaching will hit home. We may regard it as a noble and improving guide to living, but not as a salvific message. For Buddhists, rebirth is axiomatic, because it is the teaching of an enlightened mind; a mind that, in the last stages of achieving that enlightened status, actually witnessed its experience of former lives. Western Buddhists often embark on the path without fully accepting this understanding, but the important point is to trust in the Buddha's teaching – even though it may not be fully comprehensible.

The third Noble Truth: the cessation of suffering (nirodha)

Nirodha means to control. Control of the craving or thirst of attachment is the third teaching. If we accepted only the first two Noble Truths and eschewed the last two, we would have a teaching about the way things are, but no remedy for this depressing state of affairs. The first two truths diagnose the condition, but the great achievement of the Buddha was to offer a cure; therefore, as far as Buddhists are concerned, he is the physician *par excellence*.

Nirodha is the extinguishing of thirst or craving, to be achieved by rooting out attachment. It results in a state called nirvana (nibbana) in which the fires of craving have ceased to burn and there is no more suffering.

As with all illness, of course, the proposed cure is of no value unless you accept the diagnosis, so this third truth is to be understood in the light of the first two. The possibility of nirvana cannot be realized unless our present existence is understood as dukkha.

Buddhist scriptures use many metaphors to contrast dukkha and nirvana. One of the starkest is that used in the *Fire Sermon*:

The Fire Sermon
Bhikkhus, all is burning. And what is the all that is burning?
Bhikkhus, the eye is burning, visible forms are burning,
visual consciousness is burning, visual impression is
burning, also whatever sensation, pleasant or painful or
neither-pleasant-nor-painful, arises on account of the
visual impression, that too is burning. Burning with what?
Burning with the fire of lust, with the fire of hate, with the
fire of delusion; I say it is burning with birth, ageing and death,
with sorrows, with lamentations, with pains, with grief, with
despairs.

(W. Rahula, *What the Buddha Taught*, Gordon Fraser, 1982, p 95)

The Buddha recounts the same experience for all the senses, the body and the mind; he explains that one who knows this becomes dispassionate, and:

Being dispassionate, he becomes detached, through
detachment he is liberated. When liberated there is
knowledge that he is liberated. And he knows: Birth is
exhausted, the holy life has been lived, what has to be done
is done, there is no more left to be done on this account.

(W. Rahula, *What the Buddha Taught*, Gordon Fraser, 1982, pp 96–7)

Nirvana

In another darsana, he speaks of nirvana as 'getting rid of all cares and troubles' (*Sabbasava sutta*). Other poetic terms he uses include: the harbour of refuge; the cool cave; the home of ease; the place of bliss.

Here we are confronted with an apparent paradox in Buddhist thinking. If our aim is to cultivate peace, ease, bliss and well-being in ourselves, does this not make nirvana or enlightenment a selfish goal? How can it equate with the Buddha's emphasis on the extinction of self (anatta)? The Buddhist answers that this is a misunderstanding of why these goals are sought. The self is composed of self-centredness, which arises from attachment or craving. It constantly needs to be re-affirmed – and yet such reaffirmation is ultimately unattainable, because this self is a fiction. Throughout our everyday lives, we look for this affirmation from those around us. When someone praises me, I feel confident and happy. When I am blamed or deprecated, I feel anxious, even angry. When someone else is praised, I feel jealous; I experience envy. These negative states of mind are a result of attachment to my own self-centredness; even my positive states of mind depend on the same thing. In this condition, I cannot freely give and be altruistic. When we speak of cultivating nirvana it is not dependent on my self-centredness, my ego, being affirmed. It is a release from that need. In this release, it is possible to give without receiving, to offer loving kindness without first being its recipient. Freed from this flux of emotions and mental instability, I can now act freely and give when needed. I am also able to direct my attention to others' needs, rather than being preoccupied by my own. An enlightened state of mind is one in which this creative giving occurs spontaneously and without hindrance. Were the qualities inherent in an enlightened mind to be cultivated for the ego's own sake, that is, if that were the motivation, then they could not be achieved.

The fourth Noble Truth: the path to the cessation of suffering (magga)

This is known as the 'Middle Way', and avoids the two extremes of indulgence in sensual pleasures and self-mortification. It is also known as the 'Noble Eightfold Path', because it outlines eight categories through which purity of mind, calm and insight can be achieved.

These eight divisions are grouped into three aspects of Buddhist practice: Ethical Conduct (*Sila*); Mental Discipline (*Samadhi*); Wisdom (*Panna or Prajna*).

The Eightfold Path

1	Right Understanding (*Samma ditthi*)	
2	Right Intention or Orientation (*Samma sankappa*)	} Wisdom
3	Right Speech (*Samma vaca*)	
4	Right Action (*Samma kammanta*)	} Ethical Conduct
5	Right Livelihood (*Samma ajiva*)	
6	Right Effort (*Samma vayama*)	
7	Right Mindfulness (*Samma sati*)	} Mental Discipline
8	Right Concentration (*Samma samadhi*)	

As with all things in Buddhism, it is important to understand the interrelationships of these categories. The Eightfold Path is sometimes likened to a ladder with eight rungs, as though one might develop by practising each discipline in turn. This is a misleading idea, because the Buddha stressed that progress is made by the practice of each aspect of the path in concert with the others.

For example, it is important to recognize that Ethical Conduct is absolutely necessary in order to achieve Wisdom, and that without Mental Discipline we lack the capacity for Ethical Conduct. Similarly, therefore, the achievement of Compassion and Wisdom, which are the characteristics of an Enlightened One, cannot be gained separately and are not distinct. Everything goes hand in hand. The wise person is the one who acts compassionately, the compassionate person is the one who acts wisely.

One who treads the Eightfold Path is, therefore, doing something quite different from one who 'wanders' on the Wheel of Becoming. He or she recognizes the possibility of improvement and eventual emancipation and, acting on that possibility – with the Buddha's teaching and his or her own practice as the guide, alongside others who are treading the path – works creatively toward a more refined awareness of how to live well. The Eightfold Path is like a map that charts this journey.

Ethical Conduct

The Buddha said his teachings were 'for the good of the many, for the happiness of the many, out of compassion for the world'. If Ethical Conduct does not arise through following the teachings, then they are of no use whatsoever. The quality of compassion is the pinnacle of Buddhist achievement, and Ethical Conduct therefore is not an end in itself but a means to develop compassion. It is the cultivation of loving kindness, generosity and forgiveness. These qualities will manifest themselves in our activity in the world, in that which we give out in Right Speech, Right Action and Right Livelihood. To the extent that these are practised, so we will decrease the suffering of others and ourselves. We shall also purify ourselves. Understanding and practising these three aspects of the path should not be seen simply as a matter of duty and discipline. Certainly it is that, but it is more. Ultimately, such actions should become effortless and spontaneous, rather than a matter of grim resolution.

Right Speech means abstaining from telling lies, slandering and promoting division and enmity, using abusive language, and indulging in careless gossip. In some cases, if one cannot say something helpful, it is better to keep a noble silence.

Right Action promotes peaceful and harmonious conduct. It has exactly the same aims as Right Speech, but a different form of expression. Doing that which causes harm to others is its exact opposite, whether this be through taking life, stealing or taking advantage of someone sexually.

Right Livelihood determines that one should abstain from making a living through causing harm, whether by trading in arms or intoxicating drinks, killing animals or cheating.

Mental Discipline

The Buddha addressed his brethren thus: 'It is through not understanding and not grasping the Four Noble Truths, O brethren, that we have had to run for so long, to wander for so long in this weary path of transmigration, both you and I.'

The power of the Noble Truths lies in this aspect of Mental Discipline: Right Effort, Right Mindfulness and Right Concentration. Without these, nothing is attainable.

Right Effort involves preventing evil and unwholesome states of mind from arising; ridding oneself of such unwholesome states of mind that have already arisen; producing, or causing to arise, good and wholesome states of mind and bringing them to perfection. This necessitates generating the will for this to happen, and a single-minded application to the task. Without effort, which is itself an act of will, doubt, anxiety and other hindrances will distract the mind from its task.

Right Mindfulness provides the context for Right Effort. It relates it to the here and now. It is concerned with immediate states of consciousness, not speculative possibilities. It involves diligent awareness of the activities of the body, sensations and feelings; the activities of the mind, and ideas, thoughts and conceptions.

Right Concentration underpins Right Mindfulness. Without concentration, mindfulness, let alone Ethical Conduct, is impossible. Concentration is a fundamental skill, in that it develops attentiveness. In the various schools of Buddhism it is practised in different ways, but all concentrate on attention to detail, bringing the capacity of the mind to a full awareness of every thought, action and sensation. One of the basic practices is concentration on breathing (*anapanasati*). If Right Mindfulness is a matter of awareness, Right Concentration is the basis upon which that awareness is attained. Being able to be aware of the process of breathing – a fundamental physiological function – enables us to discern what is actually happening. When this concentration is applied to sensations and feelings; the activities of the mind; the ideas, thoughts and conceptions that arise and fall away in our mental habits; then a true understanding of the way things are is arrived at. It is all too easy to rationalize what is going on in ourselves as individuals, such that we affirm our desires and longings, but the antidote to this is to present ourselves with evidence for things being otherwise.

Wisdom

Wisdom consists of Right Intention or Orientation and Right Understanding. They are dependent on Right Mindfulness, as Right Thought constitutes selfless renunciation or detachment (as opposed to *attachment*, outlined previously) and Right Understanding is the realization of things as they are (as opposed to suffering the delusion that arises from pursuing desires).

Wisdom is not the result of cleverness or intellectual capacity, which are as much prey to karmic inclinations as any other capacity of mind. This is a common misreading of the Buddha's teaching, because it is presumed that following the logic of such an analytical summary of human experience necessitates great intellectual acumen. But cleverness can be as much an obstacle as it can be an aid to wisdom. It can be a tool used to proliferate self-deceit, as well as being used to cut through it. Wisdom is the summation of what has already been practised, but Right Intention or Orientation and Right Understanding are also the basis of the practice itself, as they are the motivation for Right Effort and the further aspects of the path. Clearly, therefore, wisdom can be seen as the final factor of enlightenment, but it is also cumulative; a refinement that grows as thought and understanding become progressively freed from ignorance. This unfettering is gained by practising the path as a whole. The term that sums up this process is *bhavana*, or mental development. It involves a devotional aspect, in that it is a wholehearted commitment to self-transformation. It also has a reflective aspect, in that it demands an awareness of what is happening in the here and now. It involves a highly practical aspect, in that it has a necessary purchase on the way we act in every situation. Different Buddhist movements address these forms of practice in their own particular ways, but all concur on the need to address all three.

In conclusion

In this chapter we have studied the core teachings expounded by the historical Buddha, which have been accepted as axiomatic by all his followers. However, different types of Buddhism have built on these in differing ways, which will be more fully presented later.

4

Buddhist scriptures and schools

This chapter introduces the different Buddhist scriptures and branches of Buddhism that arose after the death of the Buddha and the ways in which they developed. Like other religious traditions, Buddhism has divided into various branches over its history, and its scriptures reflect this diversity. You will learn about the differences in their teachings and ways in which new ideas developed and spread to other Asian countries, from Sri Lanka in the south to Japan in the north. The main differences in doctrine are explained and the ways in which they influenced Buddhist communities. The principle divisions in Buddhism between Theravada and Mahayana and between the Tibetan, Pure Land and Zen schools are explained. You will learn how diverse Buddhism has become, why that diversity exists, and the impact the development of Buddhism has had on the cultures in which it can be found.

After teaching for 45 years, the Buddha died at the age of 80. This is called his paranirvana, and is seen as a final release from the round of rebirth. His teachings were memorized by his followers and passed on by oral tradition. By 480 BCE, a council was called to ratify the Buddha's teachings. The aim of this council, held in Rajgir, was to agree a definitive version of the Buddha's message.

By 380 BCE, a second council was called at Vesali to ensure that the *Vinaya* – the code of discipline – was adhered to by all Buddhist monks. At this gathering, differences of opinion arose as to what the Buddha actually taught. At this point, the first division in the Buddha's followers arose. This division increased until, eventually, two main schools in Buddhism emerged. One became known as the *Mahayana*, meaning 'Great Vehicle', and the other comprised a number of more conservative groups, of which the surviving example was the *Theravada*, meaning 'Way of the Elders'. The Mahayana spread north-west from India into present-day Nepal, China, Tibet, Japan, Korea and Vietnam.

Theravada Buddhism spread southwards into Sri Lanka, Burma, Thailand, Cambodia and Laos.

The Theravada Scriptures

It is said that the first Buddhist scriptures were written down by Theravada monks at the fourth council in Sri Lanka, during the first century BCE. They used the ancient colloquial Indian language of Pali, spoken by the Buddha. The scriptures were written on palm leaves and became known as the *Pali Canon* or *Tipitaka*. The term 'tipitaka' means 'three baskets', which refers to the threefold division of the scriptures, known as *Vinaya Pitaka*, *Sutta Pitaka* and *Abhidhamma Pitaka*.

The *Tipitaka*

The *Vinaya* is the book of discipline for monks containing the 227 rules by which they must live. The *Sutta Pitaka* contains the teachings of the Buddha on the Four Noble Truths, Eightfold Path and the popular Buddhist literature that constitutes the

Dhammapada and the *Jataka Tales*. Sutta means 'thread', and indicates the connection seen to exist between the different teachings of the Buddha that constitutes the overall world view of the tradition. Dhammapada means 'Path of Truth'. It consists of an anthology of the Buddha's sayings, collected between 563 and 483 BCE. They act as a source of guidance for Buddhists everywhere but especially for those in the Theravada tradition. The *Jataka Tales* are a collection of stories of the Buddha's previous lives. They focus on the Ten Perfections, which lead to perfect Buddhahood: generosity, virtue, renunciation, wisdom, energy, patience, truthfulness, resolution, loving kindness and an even temper. The *Abhidhamma Pitaka* contains the more philosophical teachings that underpin the Buddhist understanding of life. They were intended as a basis of the Buddhist outlook, which opposed other Indian conceptions of reality. They are essentially philosophical and psychological, arguing the Buddhist perspective against other prevailing philosophical positions in the Indian sub-continent, and are the source of its doctrinal formulations.

The arahant

The highest aspiration in Theravada Buddhism is to become an *arahant* (arhat), or one who has passed beyond the fetters of samsaric existence.

> *Ah happy indeed the Arahants! In them is no craving found. The 'I am' conceit is rooted out; confusion's net is burst, lust free they have attained; translucent is the mind of them.*
>
> (*Samyutta Nikaya* III:83)

The arahant is the ideal of the Theravadin school. The word refers to those saints or sages who, having followed the Buddha's teachings, upon death, will enter into nibbana (nirvana). They are fully emancipated.

The scriptures describe an arahant by a standard formula, as one in whom the 'outflows' (sense desire, becoming, ignorance, wrong views) have 'dried up'; one who has 'done what has to be done'. However, the question remained (and later exercised Buddhist thinkers) as to the distinction between an arahant and a buddha. It was this distinction that the Mahayana school exploited, indicating that the ideal of arahantship and the goal of nibbana were inferior to the larger aspiration of buddhahood and the bodhisattva path (described later), which accentuated the virtues of compassion, and of gaining emancipation for the sake of others rather than for one's own entry into nirvana.

The Mahayana Scriptures

The spread of Buddhism in different directions resulted in a diversity of doctrines and scriptures. For the Theravadins, the authenticity of the scriptures was determined by which texts, historically, actually came from the Buddha himself. But in opposition to this, Mahayana Buddhists asserted that certain other scriptures were just as authoritative, even though they could not be traced back to the Buddha in a historical way. They claimed authority more by mythological connection than historical. For example, the *Prajna Paramita Sutras* (the teachings on Perfect Wisdom), which are scriptures of great significance in the Mahayana tradition, are said to have been revealed by the Buddha himself, but were too difficult to be understood by his contemporaries. Because of this, they were stored in the palace of the nagas (serpents) in the Nether World. When the time was right to reveal them, the great Buddhist thinker, Nagarjuna, brought them back into the human realm.

The Mahayana scriptures are written in the ancient, classical Indian language of Sanskrit. Mahayana texts vary in form and introduce both mythological and philosophical features not found in the *Theravada*. Siddhartha, the historical Buddha, often takes on a more mystical and poetic character. An important development was the Mahayana emphasis on the accessibility of other Buddhas, that he was not the only Buddha: there were others before him and others yet to come. While the Theravadins did not deny this, they didn't regard these various Buddhas as accessible in the present time. Visiting a Tibetan shrine room, one is struck by the plethora of forms of enlightened beings. These represent particular qualities or energies, and appear not in strictly naturalistic form, but expressing their symbolic significance. Thus, for example, Avalokiteshvara represents the quality of compassion, Manjushri represents the quality of wisdom.

Behind these representations is the development of doctrine, which serves to explain them.

The Bodhisattva

The *bodhisattva*, literally *bodhi* (enlightened) and *sattva* (essence), is a being who delays his entry into nirvana in order to help all sentient beings. Out of compassion, he or she returns to the samsaric realm to help others along the path.

The *Diamond Sutra* says: 'A bodhisattva is not attached to anything when he gives, like a person in the daylight who can see things as they really are.' For this reason, Mahayana Buddhists take what is called the Bodhisattva vow, which states:

The deluding passions are inexhaustible.
I vow to extinguish them all.
Sentient beings are numberless.
I vow to save them all.
The truth is impossible to expound.
I vow to expound it.
The way of the Buddha is unattainable.
I vow to attain it.

This idea is based on the teachings of the *Prajna Paramita*. The wisdom of a bodhisattva is perfect, and goes beyond the wisdom of the world. It fully understands the absence of abiding entities, such as selfhood. It is based on the notion of *sunyata*, meaning emptiness or void.

Sunyata

The *Heart Sutra* states:

In emptiness there is no form, nor feeling, nor perception, nor impulse, nor consciousness; no eye, ear, nose, tongue, body, mind; no forms, sounds, smells, tastes, touchables or objects of mind; no sight-organ elements, and so forth until we come to no mind-consciousness element.

(*Heart Sutra* 5)

Sunyata, according to the Madhyamika school of thought, central to Mahahyana Buddhism, rests on the logic of giving up all views. Views and perceptions of reality are ultimately false because they rely on conceptual constructs. Conceptual constructs rely on dualistic thinking (i.e. every construct evokes its opposite, from hot–cold to real–unreal, absolute–relative). Because this is the case, no conceptual construct can be a reflection of reality. All conceptual constructs are the creation of the samsaric mind and thus delusory. Once this is understood, the emptying of the mind of these constructs is the equivalence of what is called nirvana. *Sunyata* (emptiness) is the term given to this. It is not nihilation as that would presume the positive value of the constructs that have been negated. Rather it is the negation of the negative. From the negative (samsaric) point of view, emptiness is a lack; nirvanically, it is the apotheosis. Thus it can also be equated with what, samsarically, we lack: bliss (the contrary of disease or suffering). However, having moved beyond conceptual constructs in this realization, we have moved beyond their expression, in language. Therefore, what is being pointed to is beyond our capability to communicate linguistically. As a correlate to this understanding comes the recognition that awareness of our Buddha-nature, that synthesis of wisdom and compassion, is not developed by intellectual means alone even though the logic of the intellect has been used to expose the falsity of our conceptual constructs of the world.

The bodhisattva path is rooted in the practice of the six perfections: patience, giving, morality, vigour, meditation and wisdom.

The Three Body Doctrine

Clearly, this development of the idea of buddhahood to include the historical Buddha, buddhas of other ages, and the principle of sunyata, or voidness, needed to be systematically expounded; we find this in the Three Body (Trikaya) Doctrine.

The historical Buddha (Siddhartha Gautama) was identified as the *nirmanakaya* (form body), a particular expression in one place and time of the eternal truths of the dharma. The *dharmakaya* was identified as the eternal principle of Truth, which transcended space and time. Through meditation and devotion Buddhists came to describe images of buddhas that are not historical but that are archetypal. These are identified as *sambhogakaya* (bliss bodies). Each of these different images represents a particular aspect of the enlightenment experience. They are a more refined understanding of the nature of enlightenment than the Buddha as an historical figure, pointing to the more abstract awareness of the idea of the ultimate truth expressed in the idea of dharmakaya.

The *Lotus Sutra*

The *Lotus Sutra*, or *Lotus of the True Law* (*Saddharma Pundarika*), is often referred to by some Mahayana Buddhists as the final teaching of the Buddha, and thus has a venerated place in the Mahayana Canon. One emphasis for which it is acclaimed is its teaching on 'upaya' or 'skill in means'.

The *Lotus Sutra* explains that there are different teachings used by the Buddha to encourage the faithful to perfect buddhahood, according to their individual propensities and capacities. All the same, though there may be said to be many paths to the same goal, they all constitute aspects of one vehicle, that is, one overall path, that of the Bodhisattva Mahasattva or Great Being. However, the Lotus Sutra allows the Buddhist message to become available to all, relative to their particular capacities. It is an acknowledgement that people do not start in the same place with regard to their apprehension of the truth. In much the same way, to teach quantum physics to a child would be an unproductive way of furthering their development. This idea is explained in the *Parable of the Burning House*.

> ### The Parable of the Burning House
> *A father owns an old house which, while he is out, catches on fire. He hears his own children still playing in the house, unaware that it is burning. Absorbed in their amusement, the children pay no attention to their father calling them out of the house. He then tells them he has special carts of different kinds for each of them to play with, and encourages the children to*

run out and find them. Once out of the house and free from danger, they find the carts are all the same — but better than any of them had expected.

The burning house is the samsaric world in which, foolishly, we are absorbed, like the children. The father is the Buddha who finds a way to deliver us from our predicament through his skill in means (upaya). Firstly, he offers gifts to get the children out of the house. Secondly, he offers them their favourite carts to encourage each of them.

From the perspective of the Lotus Sutra, the inferior carts represent the early teachings of the Hinayana (lesser vehicle) which, nevertheless, were a skilful means of getting the Buddha's followers to start on the path that leads to nirvana.

The final, best cart that the children find outside the house represents the higher ideal of perfect Buddhahood, as taught in this sutra.

In his omniscience the Buddha reveals that the destiny of all creatures is buddhahood — nothing less. The most important issue is erasing the self-imposed ignorance that blinds beings from seeing the truth. Even devout Buddhists suffer this continuing blindness.

Pure Land Buddhism

When Buddhism reached China and Japan many new schools of thought developed; two of these were particularly influential: the Pure Land School and the Ch'an (Chinese) or Zen (Japanese) School.

The two *Sukhavativyuha Sutras*, written in the second century CE, describe a Pure Land (*Sukhavati*) free from suffering. Sukhavati is a spiritual realm created by the Buddha, which is conducive to spiritual progress. It is a state of bliss (sukkha) and as such is the opposite of the samsaric realm we presently inhabit, which is marked by the pervasiveness of dukkha (unsatisfactoriness). The scriptures describe the Pure Land as 'a world called Sukhavati where there is neither bodily or mental pain for living beings. The sources of happiness are innumerable.'

The *Sukhavativyuha Sutras* gave rise to a Buddhism of faith during the fifth and sixth centuries CE in China. It revolved around the Pure Land of Amitabha (Amida in Japanese) who is the Buddha of Infinite Light and Compassion. To be reborn into his Pure Land, one only has to call his name ten times at the point of death and he will appear and escort his devotee to Sukhavati. While in the present world gaining enlightenment is difficult, in death one will be helped on the path to that goal.

This is a Buddhism of Faith, in which the principal means of salvation is the invocation of the name of the Buddha, which will ensure attainment of a state from which there is no falling back. Its popularity was rooted in its ranking equally with more rigorous meditative practices and lifestyles through which wisdom was accomplished. For many lay Buddhists, especially those whose situations in life and possibilities of education were limited, this provided a suitable path. It also emphasized the Mahayanist teaching on the universality of salvation, because scholarly progress and monasticism were no longer required.

The Ch'an and Zen Schools

Ch'an (Chinese) and Zen (Japanese) are derived from the Indian word *dhyana*, which refers to meditation. As Buddhism extended into China, then Japan, so the meditation school developed from the teachings and practice of the sixth-century Indian monk, Bodhidharma. Ironically, Bodhidharma's message was that the tradition had become too attached to the scriptures, and that the Buddha's teaching was understood by simply watching the mind or looking into one's own heart (hence the emphasis on meditation, seen as a stripping away of external trappings). Such simplicity of expression was well-suited to a Chinese culture much influenced by Taoist philosophy, which also emphasized a one-pointedness of mind, a seeing to the heart of the matter within our everyday life but beyond our everyday understanding, as this verse illustrates:

> *Thirty spokes share one hub.*
> *Adapt the nothing therein to the purpose in hand, and you will have the use of the cart.*
> *Knead clay in order to make a vessel.*
> *Adapt the nothing therein to the purpose in hand, and you will have the use of the vessel.*
> *Cut out doors and windows in order to make a room.*
> *Adapt the nothing therein to the purpose in hand, and you will have the use of the room.*
> *Thus what we gain is Something, yet it is by virtue of Nothing that this can be put to use.*

(Lao Tzu, *Tao Te Ching*, Penguin, 1968, p 67)

This represented a rigorous refusal to indulge in scriptural study or philosophical debate, in favour of a purely intuitive approach to enlightenment. Though the meditation school appeals to scripture to ground its practices in the authority of the Buddha, it does so only to support the efficacy of meditation as an end in itself, as the truth realized in action.

'Directly pointing to the mind' and 'becoming a Buddha just as you are' involves doing away with all thought, which is the means of attachment to the external world. The effect of this is to see into one's own Buddha-nature, which is obscured by defilements and attachments. Enlightenment may come suddenly or gradually. Either way, the intuiting of Truth involves the cultivation of the mind so that it is in sharp focus and constantly alert. Thus moments of pure awareness (*satori*) arise. As it developed, the meditation tradition identified patriarchs, enlightened teachers who developed their own techniques for training their pupils and became founders of branches of the tradition. These techniques were often novel and unorthodox. For example, the followers of Lin-Chi used the 'lightning' method of scolding and beating disciples. Ts'ao-tung masters preferred the question-and-answer method, whereby the disciple would be interviewed by his master to test his capacity to intuit the truth.

Characteristic of Zen is the refusal to give 'right answers', as though truth can be passed on just by hearing or reading a teaching. The master's skill lies in knowing exactly what the disciple requires to free his or her mind from attachment. Attachment may come in many forms and the mind can be freed from particular attachments in many ways. Zen stories (mondos) catalogue this highly practical method of teaching.

The Tibetan Scriptures

Buddhism entered Tibet around 650 CE, but it was not until a century later that it overcame fierce resistance from the indigenous Bon religion, with its shamanic heritage and patronage of the Tibetan nobility. In Tibet, once patronage moved from Bon to Buddhism, it flourished under the reign of Ral-pa-can (817–36 CE). Monasteries and temples were erected, and teachers were brought from India, which propagated the translation of the scriptures.

The relationship with the Bon tradition was not wholly one of animosity, and Padmasambhava, one of the most revered of Tibetan saints, did much as an Indian missionary to realign hostile forces, through his particular interpretation of practices and teachings. Buddhism also entered Tibet from China, though its impact was less successful; the character of Tibetan Buddhism illustrates Indian influence rather than Chinese.

There are four main Tibetan traditions alive today: the Nyingma, Kagya, Sakya and Geluk, each of which possess a wealth of oral and written teachings. The scriptures are classified under the following titles: the *Kangyur*, meaning 'the translation of the word', which are discourses attributed to the historical Buddha; and the *Tengyur*, which are the *shastras* (commentaries on the original teachings, translated from Indian originals). In addition to these, numerous explanatory works were written in Tibetan.

The importance of Tibetan Buddhism and its scriptures is not so much that it is specifically Tibetan, but that a great deal of the corpus of Mahayana Buddhist literature, and the maintenance of its tradition, would not have survived had it not been harboured in Tibet.

A preoccupation of Tibetan teaching is the relationship between life and death. This arises mainly due to the significance of tantric teaching in Tibetan tradition. *Tantra* represents the quick path to enlightenment in one lifetime, by grasping the opportunity of a human birth not to be wasted. It also stresses the importance of confronting our negative impulses and fears during this rebirth. Death is seen as the ultimate fear or barrier, because it represents an annihilation of our identity (as we perceive it). *The Tibetan Book of the Dead* attains an especial importance, as it deals with how to find our way through the period between death and rebirth. This concept is referred to as the 'Art of Dying', which is seen as the most significant liberating experience in Tibetan Buddhist terms.

The Tibetans understand there to be a state between dying and being reborn, referred to as the *bardo* state. During this time, the individual will follow a course that leads to liberation or a consequent rebirth according to his or her attachments. This journey is dependent on our last thoughts in our present life, and the course that they initiate, rather like a train of thought that is pursued, from its inception in thinking about either positive or negative impulses (for example, a day when we wake up with a negative or positive frame of mind). It is claimed that reading *The Tibetan Book of the Dead* to a dying person will initiate them into the process of dying in a positive frame of mind, and therefore ensure either a positive rebirth or freedom from rebirth entirely. Aldous Huxley is one Westerner who adhered to this philosophy and followed its practice, despite the adverse criticism that ensued from the United States press and subsequent biographies.

The Buddhist rationale for such a practice is that our past thinking has determined our present status, and our present thinking will determine our future status. This is rooted in scriptural understanding and the significance of karmic influence. What *The Tibetan Book of the Dead* (*Bardo Thodol*) points to is the most significant event in our lives – our own demise – for which we have a whole lifetime either to prepare for or to ignore. It indicates the importance of preparation for the ultimate test of our earthly achievement, when all else that we rely on has passed: status, reputation and other worldly successes. We are left only with our own mind, naked and unprotected. At this point the practice of the teaching bears fruit:

> *O now when the Dhyana Bardo upon me is dawning!*
> *Abandoning the whole mass of distractions and illusions,*
> *May the mind be kept in the mood of endless undistracted Samadhi,*
> *May firmness both in the visualizing and in the perfected stages be obtained:*
> *At this time, when meditating one-pointedly, with all other actions put aside,*
> *May I not fall under the power of misleading, stupifying passions.*

> (W.Y. Evans-Wentz, *The Tibetan Book of the Dead*,
> Oxford University Press, 1960, p 203)

In conclusion

This chapter has introduced the various scriptures and schools in Buddhism and identified their salient features and differences. As a result we can now consider the following significant factors in the development of Buddhism:

* the central role of the bodhisattva in Mahayana Buddhism as a salvific force and how this contrasted with the arahant ideal in Theravada
* the introduction of a Buddhism of faith within Chinese and Japanese culture
* the influence of Taoism on Chinese and Japanese Buddhism, moving it in a contrasting dection based on mystical intuition
* the Tibetan interpretation of Buddhism, involving the need of a spiritual guide, and an emphasis on the preparation for death.

5

meditation and devotion

This chapter introduces the distinctive spiritual practices of Buddhism, the reasons for them and their effects. It shows how the cultivation of mindfulness underpins various Buddhist meditation techniques and how calm and insight are promoted through different types of meditation. Links are made to the teachings of the Eightfold Path showing how teachings and practices are intimately related. You will learn how some practices are more devotional in nature and how these are practised in specific branches of Buddhism. Visualization and bowing are examined to explain how Buddhism understands the relationship between heart and mind and how spiritual practice is used to cultivate loving kindness, compassion and wisdom. Meditation and devotional practice are regarded as essential in Buddhism in order to make progress in treading the path. You will learn how these practices are carried out and the way in which they are meant to influence behaviour in everyday life.

Mindfulness and concentration

Ayya Khema, a Buddhist nun, writes:

During meditation we learn to drop from the mind what we don't want to keep. We only want to keep in mind our meditation subject. As we become more and more skilled at it, we start to use the same faculty in our daily lives to help us drop those thoughts which are unwholesome. In this way our meditation practice assists us in daily living and our attention to wholesome thoughts in everyday life helps our meditation practice. The person who becomes master of his or her own thoughts and learns to think what they want to think is called an Arahant, an Enlightened One.

(Ayya Khema, *Being Nobody, Going Nowhere*,
Wisdom Publications, 1987, p 11)

Formal meditation practice is like exercising the mind in the same way as we might exercise the body – in order to keep it fit and healthy, and to improve its function for a specific purpose. The basic function of the mind is concentration. Right Concentration is the eighth step of the Path, but this does not mean it is the one that comes last. Rather, we have to think of the eight steps as the development of skilfulness in eight aspects that go hand in hand, like a progressive and interdependent evolution. Most importantly, without Right Concentration, Right Mindfulness is unattainable. Thus basic exercises of concentration are the foundation of meditation. But concentration on what? The most widely used traditional practice is called mindfulness of, or concentration on, breathing (*anapanasati*).

Mindfulness of the breath

The breath is a good focus for such a meditational exercise because it is neutral. As a bodily function it usually escapes our attention, since it does not give rise to pleasant or unpleasant sensations, nor does it excite the mind. Because we take it for granted we also overlook its significance, in much the same way as we do with a life-giving substance like water. Yet it is the basis of life. Equally, its relationship with the mind is direct in a physiological and emotional sense. Breath provides oxygen, through which the mind functions. In a state of excitement we breathe fast; in a state of calm and tranquility, we breathe slowly. The breath is therefore an indicator of our mental state.

We can concentrate on the breath at various points: as it goes into and exits from the body, by concentrating on the sensation of it passing through the nostrils; by following its passage down to and returning from the abdomen; by accompanying each breath cycle with a word, such as 'Buddho' (a reminder of the relationship between concentration and enlightenment); by counting breaths, one on the in-breath, two on the out-breath, and so on up to ten.

With increasing concentration the mind becomes more tranquil, and its activity diminishes. In a state of pure calm, an awareness arises of the present moment that is undisturbed, and with it arises a moment of bliss, a lack of anxiety. When the mind is in this state, its energy is available for the purposes for which we choose to use it, unhampered by negative feelings.

Calm and insight

Insight is the goal; calm is the means. Many images have been used to illustrate this. One is of the sea, both in its calm state and in a storm. The calm sea is tranquil and serene, not only in itself, but in the effect it has upon us. Similarly, waves, foam and the sea's roar in a storm are exciting, powerful and fearful. The calm sea is like the calm mind. The stormy sea is a mind in turmoil. When the sea is calm we can see through it, but in its rough state, nothing below the surface can be seen. This ability to see below the surface is insight. We see with clarity and penetration.

Meditational techniques

Accordingly, meditational techniques are divided into two types: *samatha*, which means calm; and *vipassana*, which means insight. Insight means knowing what is really happening in our minds and in our relations with others, and doing our best to create a harmonious situation in every circumstance. The significance of insight may best be described by showing how it can be obscured by negative feelings arising in the present moment. I come to each situation in a particular state of mind. Sometimes, when depressed, sad or sorrowful, I greet people in this particular state, and it colours my impression of them and the way I feel about them. This is essentially a preoccupation with myself that interferes with my concern for others and their well-being, but I say, 'I cannot help it'. Such states can be self-perpetuating and gather momentum. In my morose condition, the happy person is someone to be envied. I cannot share in their happiness and, inevitably, this shows. Then I complain about losing friends or not being wanted, and the downward spiral continues. If someone says, 'cheer up', or, 'it is not as bad as it seems', I feel even worse! Insight is the recognition of what is going on in our minds when these feelings arise, so that we may prevent ourselves from slipping back into similar mental habits time and time again. Mindfulness creates the opportunity to change these habits, by letting go of our attachment to them.

The first step on this path is to recognize such thoughts and feelings as delusion. Not because they do not exist, but because they do not constitute our 'selves'. They are not 'me', but phenomena that arise and pass away. This is the truth of impermanence that vipassana meditation makes clear. Nothing abides, nothing has to be held onto. Without this awareness the mind manipulates us, like a magician, into believing the illusions that our thoughts convey; these illusions in turn cause us distress and separate us from others.

For this reason, every sensation is a matter for awareness: those of the body, and feelings and thoughts.

Metta

Another important Buddhist teaching is that one should be a blessing to the world. There is a Zen picture of a bodhisattva, who wanders with his staff visiting villages, depicted standing, smiling with children around him. The legend that accompanies the picture explains that he enters the village with bliss-bestowing hands. This expresses the purpose of what is aspired to in the Buddhist life.

Metta is the word that sums up this state of being. The *Metta-sutta*, the teaching on universal love or loving-kindness, proclaims that:

> *Whatever beings there may be – feeble or strong, long (or tall), stout or medium or short, small or large, seen or unseen, those dwelling far or near, those who are born and those who are yet to be born – may all beings, without exception, be happy-minded.*

Mettabhavana

This undiscriminating attitude is cultivated in a popular meditation (*mettabhavana*). It consists of five stages. In the first, one generates metta for oneself. (This is not a self-love in the sense of self-appreciation as a special person, above others, but a recognition of one's capacity to be loving to others and loveable.) At this stage one repeats: 'May I be well, may I be happy, may I progress.' In the second stage the feeling is extended to a friend, in the third stage to a neutral person, in the fourth to someone towards whom you have antipathy. In the fifth you see all these together, and then visualize the whole world of living beings and extend metta to all of them.

Visualization

The skill of visualization is a way both of concentrating the mind and of developing the quality of compassion. One Buddhist writer explains:

> *For our efforts at the spiritual life to be crowned with success not only do we need to be intellectually convinced by Buddhism, but we also need to find it emotionally attractive. We need both Truth and Beauty. Images, especially beautiful images, involve our emotions in the spiritual life and thereby make it possible for us actually to live it.*

> (*FWBO Newsletter*, No. 56, 1982, p 12)

Visualization is not just a development of our imagination, but a focusing of our inherent qualities for transforming ourselves and the world, through 'seeing with the mind's eye'. It emancipates us from the effect of negative emotions, thus enabling us to respond more effectively to difficult situations. Essentially, it means that by visualizing the form of a bodhisattva (a being with higher qualities), we let go of our egotistical desires and our selfhood, and are therefore able to act in the world in a more beneficial way.

Bowing to the Buddha

Buddhists participate in *pujas*, which is an Indian word for formal worship. When Buddhists enter a temple or shrine room in which an image of a buddha is installed, they may go before the image, kneel down and bow three times so that their forehead touches the floor. This is a very formal action. The three bows represent the Buddha, dhamma and sangha.

Tibetan Buddhists often prostrate themselves (an extension of bowing), by lying full length on the floor with the head pointing towards the image. Such a ritual (rather like the act of offering flowers, candles and incense which are traditional Buddhist offerings) acts as a reminder of commitment to an ideal, and a way of bringing oneself closer to that ideal.

When Buddhists bow or make offerings, they should genuinely recognize that they aspire to progress by recognizing that the ideal lies beyond them in the present, but that it is attainable.

Nam-myoho-renge-kyo

In Nichiren Buddhism we meet another form of devotion based on the title of the Lotus Sutra which, in Chinese, is rendered as Myoho-renge-kyo. Devotion, or dedication, consists in the recitation of this mantra daily in order for the reciter to attain Buddhahood in their lifetime. This can be understood as a form of prayer which is not

> *for the protection of the gods and Buddhas who stand above and control men. Rather the intensified spiritual force of life which forms our strong prayers reveals itself as the power of faith and the power of practice. These two powers induce the power of the Buddha and the power of the Law to function*

*within us ... Prayer is something which causes a change in the
depths of a human heart.*

(Daisaku Ikeda, 'On Prayer', in Jim Cowan (ed.), *The Buddhism of the Sun*,
Richmond, UK, NSUK, 1982, p 71)

In this understanding, it is the power of the Buddha and
Law which, when invoked by faith and dedicated practice, will
necessarily secure salvation.

Namu Amida Butsu

In a similar way, in Pure Land Buddhism it is stated by the
Buddha Amitabha (Amida) in this scripture that:

*if those beings who in immeasurable and innumerable Buddha
countries, after they have heard my name ... should direct
their thought to be born in that Buddha country of mine ... if
these should not be born in that Buddha country, even those
who have only ten times repeated the thought ... then may
I not obtain the highest perfect knowledge.*

(The Larger Sukhavati-Vyuha, verse 19, in Cowell, E.B. (ed.),
Buddhist Mahayana Texts, Part 11, Oxford, Dover, 1969, p 15)

One of the great teachers of Pure Land Buddhism, Honen,
defined this form of worship in his 'One Sheet of Paper' as being
'nothing but the mere repetition of the Namu Amida Butsu without
a doubt of his mercy whereby one may be born into Paradise'
(Sir Charles Eliot, 1969, *Japanese Buddhism*, New York, Routledge
and Kegan Paul, p 365).

Here again, devotion is rewarded on the grounds that the
power of that invoked is sufficient to ensure salvation or liberation,
rather than that the efforts of those seeking it are, in themselves,
sufficient.

In conclusion

In this chapter, we have examined different approaches to
meditation and devotion in Buddhist practice.

ethical conduct

This chapter explains the way in which Buddhists understand ethics and how that is related to the teachings in the Eightfold Path, the precepts and meditation and devotion. It introduces the idea of skillfulness or skill in means to show how one has to have the right intention but also be skillful in carrying it out. You will learn how Buddhist ethics is about working on oneself with the aim of having a positive influence in the world and being of benefit to others. Renunciation is explained as not just giving up material things but giving up self-centeredness so that one can give kindness. The chapter focuses on the practical nature of Buddhist ethics grounded in the idea that ethics has no value if it does not result in positive change to the way things are done and the way we live.

Sila and skilfulness

Sila is the Buddhist term for ethical or moral behaviour, which is summed up in the three connected ethical steps of the Eightfold Path (Right Speech, Right Action, Right Livelihood, referred to in Chapter 3). At the same time, an emphasis on living well pervades Buddhist teaching and practice. This is expressed in an obvious way, in the precepts which provide everyday guidance in a simple form (simple to remember, that is, rather than simple to keep). But in order to keep the precepts successfully, Buddhists recognize the need for sustained development in themselves. We could say that the precepts provide a practical framework, for us to be guided by in our everyday activity, but the intention is to try to keep them. This intention and effort are all important, otherwise no progress can be made. Behind the precepts encompassing them is the Eightfold Path, which informs Buddhists as to how this can be achieved. Bhavana, or mental development, is what lies beneath the surface, what is happening within the person that creates this possibility. The aspiration at the heart of this is skilfulness, its effect in the world and on others – this is the cultivation of happiness and harmony.

The practicality of Buddhist ethics

Looking at Buddhist ethics in this way affirms the importance of addressing a pervasive misconception that is often held about the relevance of ethics, and the relevance of Buddhist ideas to everyday life. Both can be separated from our daily activity and treated as intellectual mind-games, but this is not the intention. The purchase of both is their utility: do they make a difference to the way we live and the world we create? This question tests their efficacy and, at the same time, helps us penetrate what otherwise may seem baffling and remote concepts. For example, the significance of anatta, the doctrine of no-self, involves an awareness only gained by the practice of mindfulness. In turn, mindfulness makes us increasingly aware of the heedlessness of much of our thought and actions. In this way, Right Speech, Action and Livelihood gain a practical significance that we can illustrate from reflection on our experience. Ignorance ceases to be a question of lack of theoretical knowledge; we can put our finger on exactly when it has determined the way we have behaved. Furthermore, we begin to realize that the view of ourselves that has prompted such actions (composed of desire and aversion) is the delusion that ensures this unsatisfactory state of affairs is maintained and replayed.

This analysis helps us to realize also that the Buddhist emphasis on intention is not about having the right sentiments or ignoring the effect of what we do. Buddhist morality is not a soft option based upon the wish to be a nice person or do good works. There is a rigour in Buddhist morality, because it conjoins both our intelligence, in the fullest sense of the term, and our feelings, in relation to what we will for ourselves and others, in progressing toward wisdom and compassion. This is why skilfulness plays such a central role, as the following Buddhist writer explains:

> *According to Buddhist tradition there are two kinds of action, kausalya (Pali kusala) or skilful, and akausalya (Pali akusala) or unskilful. This is significant because the terms 'skilful' and 'unskilful', unlike the terms 'good' and 'bad', suggest that morality is very much a matter of intelligence. You cannot be skilful unless you can understand things, unless you can see possibilities and explore them. Hence morality, according to Buddhism, is as much a matter of intelligence and insight as one of good intentions and good feelings. After all, we have been told that the path to hell is paved with good intentions, but you could hardly say that the path to hell is paved with skilfulness. It just doesn't fit.*

> (Sangharakshita, *A Guide to the Buddhist Path*,
> Windhorse Publications, 1990, p 140)

We can now see the moral sense of what appear at first to be simply abstract logical formulations, for example, the bare doctrinal formulation of cause and effect.

That being thus this comes to be;
from the coming to be of that, this arises;
that being absent, this does not happen;
from the cessation of that, this ceases.

(Majjhima Nikaya, Vol. II, quoted in H. Saddhatissa, *Buddhist Ethics*,

Wisdom Publications, 1987, p 28)

This can now be applied on both the grand scale (spelt out in the theory of karma), and also in the minutiae of thought and action between one moment and the next.

Working on yourself and benefiting others

'Working on yourself' in terms of awareness and discipline is of fundamental importance but, from a Western point of view, coloured by our own cultural context, it can appear to have an individualistic emphasis, contrasting thinking of others with thinking of oneself. If this is also related to the traditional Buddhist communal form of monasticism, then it might appear as a retreat from social obligation; a form of self-obsession and introversion. But this is not the case. Self-development and the recognition of personal and social responsibility are inseparable. The principle holds good on the individual and the global scales; what matters is to keep the balance. In traditional Buddhist countries, the balance is kept by regarding monastic and lay life as interdependent aspects of the social order. In the West, we have some difficulty with this, due to a very different social history. Nevertheless, it is important to consider what external environment, what pattern of daily life and what time spent in quietude to address issues, is necessary.

The precepts and the dharmas

The precepts outline what to abstain from, and the dharmas are the qualities to cultivate. They go together, and it is important to recognize that while abstaining from the one negative state of mind resulting in negative action, the other, positive, state is encouraged. The precepts have already been mentioned in Chapter 1.

The basic dharmas

The basic dharmas, or ethical principles, are also five in number:
* Abstaining from acts of harmfulness is an encouragement of metta, or loving kindness.
* Abstaining from taking what is not given is an encouragement of *dana*, or generosity.
* Abstaining from sexual misconduct is an encouragement of *santutthi*, or contentment.
* Abstaining from false speech is an encouragement of *sacca*, or truthfulness.
* Abstaining from intoxicants of the mind is an encouragement of *sati*, mindfulness or awareness.

Here, then, is the foundation of Buddhist practice (bhavana), the qualities without which no progress is possible. The precepts are held up as the fundamental code of Buddhist ethical life, not because they stop you doing what you might want, but because only to the extent that they are adhered to can the discipline required to progress be made possible.

Buddhism does not, of course, simply think in terms of individual ethics. A question that is often asked, especially by individuals who feel disempowered, is 'What can I do to change the whole situation?' Wars, famines and global catastrophes constantly confront us, in the news and in the media generally. While we need to know about such events, we also have to feel able to respond to them, rather than retreat from them. In this respect, the first precept is particularly significant. Most religious and ethical traditions make firm statements about not killing in a needless way, not murdering and abjuring senseless violence. But the first precept, abstention from harming living beings, is a commitment to non-violence. While in theory this is a very noble aim, we would be mistaken to say that it is not contentious.

So we start with the situation we find ourselves in, and accept that we are working on ourselves to influence the overall world that we live in, with the aspiration to be virtuous in all things. Ultimately this aspiration is to achieve harmlessness, but at present it is to be as kind as possible.

Renunciation

No account of Buddhist morality would be complete without dwelling on the concept of renunciation, which is so central to the Buddhist view. It is apt to be misunderstood when it is seen as a curtailment of freedom and opportunity, but this is largely due to a reductionist understanding of such a rich concept. The important question is, 'What does renunciation entail?'

Once the Buddha had set in motion the Wheel of the Law (dharma) by preaching his first sermon, he spoke of having entered on the course that will make an end of suffering, and he stated that, 'The road was declared by me when I had understood the removal of the darts.'

The darts (*salla*) are the hindrances or fetters that bind us to the round of rebirth. They symbolize lust, hatred, delusion, pride, false views, grief and indecision. When Buddhists speak about renunciation, it is in relation to these things. Buddhist decisions about morality are necessarily undertaken with the knowledge that virtue itself lies in the renunciation of these things, and that whatever situation arises, Right Action or Livelihood cannot be motivated by any of these forces. While in humanitarian terms we may recognize fairness, or even retribution, as a way of dealing with the balance of events in life (on a personal or global scale), that course can never be the proper motivation of a Buddhist sensibility. Whatever takes place here and now is determined by the ongoing effect of karmic conditioning, and the eradication of this can only be initiated by the renunciant ideal. A short-term re-balancing of affairs, from a moral point of view, is not necessarily an improvement in the overall context of human history. We may witness this in the fact that the ending of one war or period of violence does not end violence altogether. The seeds of one conflict may be sown in the conclusion of a previous one. Necessarily, therefore, the ideal of renunciation has to take account of the continuous possibility of present suffering, while holding fast to the motivation that renunciation imposes. As with all ethical ideals found within the great religious traditions, the conflict between pragmatism and idealism is pronounced; but Buddhism, perhaps, identifies it more obviously than others, as renunciation brooks no compromise. Its strength lies in its overall vision but, understandably, this involves a commitment that is not easy to sustain.

In conclusion

You will have noted how Buddhist ethics dwell on practicalities and attention to the everyday, and a process of improving our sensitivity in the way we live and treat others, both humans and other creatures. In looking forward to the next chapter on moral issues, it is worth noting that from a Buddhist perspective:

* There are no absolute laws, only principles to be borne in mind. There is no absolute authority or set of commandments handed down by a divine being. There is no idea of punishment, only the karmic injunction that you reap what you sow in terms of both the effects you create in the world and the concomitant effects you create for yourself.

7

moral issues

This chapter introduces a number of important contemporary moral issues and discusses Buddhist teachings in these contexts: animal welfare, ecology, vegetarianism, capital punishment, abortion and mercy killing, and gender and equality. In each case, it applies Buddhist ethical principles and shows different views that Buddhists have developed in relation to the issues posed. You will learn how, within the framework of the teachings and practice, a stress is placed on individual responsibility, the importance of compassion and the welfare of all beings. In some cases, this has resulted in Buddhist views changing as societies have also changed their norms and values. It is possible for some Buddhists to hold differing views to those of others. In some cases, for example, with regard to vegetarianism and gender equality, Buddhists in the West are re-evaluating traditional norms.

For Buddhists, all moral issues are approached with the following in mind:

* purifying the mind and developing wisdom
* following the precepts
* the law of karma and rebirth
* intentionality and skilfulness
* developing loving kindness and compassion.

These are not separate considerations but rather the factors that ensure that what one does is a blessing to the world, rather than a corruption of it. Sila (ethical action) is the expression of dharma (truth); carried out in the course of everyday life and moral decision making, it frees the world from disease and confusion.

However, for Buddhists, there is no overall authority that legislates right and wrong on particular issues. There is guidance, and there are limits, but the task of making difficult decisions, within the framework of the precepts, is the individual's responsibility. The following issues have been chosen to illustrate this, and to represent particular focuses of Buddhist concern.

The natural world

Animal welfare

Rebirth, when aligned to the doctrine of harmlessness, leads Buddhists to emphasize compassionate attitudes to all living things. The *Buddhist Declaration on Nature* affirms:

The fact that (animals) may be incapable of communicating their feelings is no more an indication of apathy or insensibility to suffering or happiness than in the case of a person whose faculty of speech is impaired ...

There is a striking similarity between exterminating the life of a wild animal for fun and terminating the life of an innocent human being at the whim of a more capable and powerful person ... [Buddhism is a] system which propagates the theory of rebirth and life after death, it maintains that in the continuous birth and rebirth of sentient beings (not only on this planet but in the universe as a whole) each being is related to us ourselves, just as our own parents are related to us in this life ...

(*Buddhist Declaration on Nature*, Assisi, 29 September 1986)

Ecology

The Buddhist emphasis on harmony and ecological balance is extended to the whole of the natural world. Buddhists see a need to ensure the balance of nature as an ethical priority. In the *Buddhist Declaration on Nature* at the Conference of World Faiths in Assisi, they stated:

Hence Buddhism is a religion of love, understanding and compassion, and committed towards the ideal of non-violence. As such, it also attaches great importance to wildlife and the protection of the environment on which every being in this world depends for survival.

In the West, where ecological issues have gained some prominence, Buddhist initiatives have also been in evidence. For example, in 1979, The English Sangha Trust bought an area of West Sussex woodland for a Forest Retreat Sangha. This is now the focus of a conservation project based on the Buddhist idea of harmony with all forms of life. The wood is being restored to its original character – having previously been exploited commercially – by the implementation of a monocultural system of agriculture, wherein are planted trees of a species suitable for growing as a cash crop. The wood is now seen as a place of peace and tranquillity, where monks and nuns can engage in solitary meditation and retreat, and where indigenous wildlife can flourish.

Vegetarianism

Given the first precept, it might seem logical that all Buddhists are vegetarian; however, this is not always the case.

Vegetarians would maintain that meat-eating represents a tacit acceptance of human greed, and a complicity in its process. So, one may ask, should Buddhists not therefore align themselves with the principle of vegetarianism?

Of course, the principle of rebirth also plays a part in this argument. In Mahayana Buddhism, one of the themes for contemplation is that, in the endless cycle of rebirths, not a single being has not been our mother, father, husband or other relative in some way. This breaks down the species division between humans and non-humans, and does not allow us to think of other creatures as separate, inferior life forms. All life therefore becomes sacred.

Nevertheless, traditionally, Buddhism is not exclusively vegetarian. One contemporary Buddhist, of the Tibetan tradition, in answer to the question 'May monks eat meat?' replies:

> *Strictly speaking, from the point of view of the* **vinaya***, a monk should not eat meat. However, most Tibetan monks do eat meat and I have been influenced by them so I eat it too. Originally, when I was first ordained and living in a monastery in Nepal most of my time was spent in study and meditation so I didn't eat meat. We tended to get up early and go to bed early and a vegetarian diet made sleep lighter and the mind clearer for meditation. But when I started travelling and leading a more 'normal' lifestyle – working – I just found that I was too hungry at night and did not feel so strong. So I started eating meat.*

> (P. Connolly and C. Erricker, *The Presence & Practice of Buddhism*, West Sussex Institute of Higher Education, 1985, p 111)

So the answer to the question, 'Are Buddhists vegetarian?' is this: some are and some are not. However, Western Buddhists are certainly sensitive to this issue, and many see a sensitizing of our way of life as a commitment to vegetarianism.

Human society

Capital punishment

In principle, and following the first precept, Buddhism deplores the taking of life under any circumstances. However, in some Buddhist countries, notably Thailand and Burma, the death penalty is exercised in certain cases. One of the most important teachers ·

in Buddhist history, Buddhaghosa, considered the act of killing and murder as follows:

> *'Taking life' means to kill anything that lives. The precept says that you should not strike or kill any living being. 'Anything that lives' is anything that has what is called the 'life-force'. This includes all members of the animal kingdoms as well as humans. 'Taking life' means killing or trying to kill deliberately, by word or action.*
>
> *With regard to animals, it is worse to kill large ones than small ones. This is because you have to make a much greater effort to kill large ones. Even where the effort is the same, the difference in importance has to be taken into account. When it comes to human beings, the killing is considered to be worse if the person killed was a good (virtuous) person. Apart from that, the seriousness of the offence is also measured by how much the murderer wanted the killing to happen.*

(quoted in J.Rankin et al., *Religion and Ethics*, Longman, 1991, p 152)

While the act of killing is effectively prohibited in principle, the important issue is to be compassionate in any circumstance. Given this, one should offer this compassion to anyone, whatever their circumstance and whatever acts they may have committed.

Abortion and mercy killing

In this area, the Five Precepts once more prevail as guiding principles – especially the first, which is linked with the quality of compassion. However, given that there is no overriding authority in ethical matters in Buddhism, each individual must make his or her own decision about the circumstances in which they find themselves.

Abortion, in principle, is to be avoided, though, as the following comment shows, it is not absolutely forbidden:

> *Although abortion appears to, perhaps really does, abrogate the first principle, it might on balance, and in particular circumstances, yet be considered a necessity for compassionate reasons.*

(General Secretary, The Buddhist Society)

However, groups motivated by the Buddhist principle of compassion do tend to attach a particular significance to birth — despite it not being linked to a doctrine of creation — as is demonstrated here with regard to doctors and midwives:

> *Every birth is Holy. I think that a midwife must be religious, because the energy she is dealing with is Holy. She needs to know that other people's energy is sacred.*

(Ina May Gaskin, *Spiritual Midwifery*, The Book Publishing Co., 1980, p 282)

Gender and equality

In all the major religious traditions of the world this is a vexed issue, largely for historical and social reasons. In the times of those who founded traditions, the status of women tended to be subservient to that of men. In Indian culture, the caste system provided a rigorous definition of a woman's role. For example, the question of a dowry, to be paid by the wife's parents to those of the husband, was also an indication of what was expected of her in the future.

In Buddhism the caste system was abolished, even though the monastic nature of the movement made the Buddha reticent to receive women into the order. The segregation of males and females was strictly observed in the context of renunciation, which emphasized the importance of avoiding situations that could inflame lustful desires.

However, women were accepted in both lay and monastic environments. The role of the mother, as one who gave and who was worthy of compassion, was stressed. The notion of rebirth actually accentuated the recognition that gender difference was not a fundamental determinant of identity. As the tradition evolved, so women played their part. When Buddhism extended beyond India to Sri Lanka, an order of nuns was requested for the island. Nevertheless, conservative social influences have tended to ensure that, on the whole, the role of women in traditionally Buddhist countries today is not equal to that of men, whether in the monastic sangha or lay life. In the Theravadin tradition, there is some difficulty regarding the status of nuns, as full ordination died out in the lineage over the course of time, and Western female Buddhists who decide to take up the monastic life are duly prevented from achieving fully ordained status. Therefore they are, at present, subservient in status to any ordained monk, regardless of the number of years they have been in the sangha. This is an issue that the Western branches of Theravada Buddhism are constantly seeking to address.

In other branches of Buddhism, the issue has evolved differently. A woman was made spiritual head of the reformed Soto-Zen Church, as Abbess of Shasta Abbey in California, and Throssel Hole Priory in the United Kingdom. The Reverend Jiyu-Kennett was certified as Dharma Heir and fully licensed teacher by her master, the Very Reverend Keido Chisan Koho, Zenji.

As far as equality is concerned, there is still a way to go, but Western Buddhism could provide the lead in this respect, because it is such a significant issue in Western society.

In conclusion

In this chapter, we have covered Buddhist responses to a number of moral issues. However, as noted in the previous chapter, Buddhism does not have a systematic philosophy of ethics, as a result:

* While there is a rich tradition of moral reasoning in Buddhism, it is not possible to state 'what Buddhism teaches' about specific moral issues. The emphasis on 'moral enquiry' in Buddhist tradition tends to set up something equivalent to a 'case law' to be drawn upon, rather than absolute injunctions. Because Buddhist approaches to moral issues are based upon applying a principle, such as compassion, to a situation, it is possible for the outcome (the action taken or not taken) to vary. In this respect we could classify Buddhist morality as being 'situational' rather than rule abiding.

the social order

This chapter presents Buddhist understandings of different social structures and institutions. It also considers life-cycle rituals within which Buddhists are involved. Because Buddhism is traditionally a religion within which monasticism is highly significant, ordination and celibacy are discussed. You will also learn about weddings and marriage, family life and birth and upbringing. In particular, Buddhist approaches to death and dying are discussed because of the Buddhist emphasis on rebirth and, in the case of revered Buddhist figures who are believed to be enlightened, such as the Dalai Lama, the need to find them in their reborn form.

Ordination

Ordination generally entails taking up the mendicant life and 'going forth' as a monk or nun. In the Theravada tradition this is known as *bhikkhu ordination*, and follows on from the procedure first established by the Buddha when he ordained his first disciples, saying, '*Ehi bhikkhu!*' ('*come bhikkhu!*') after his first sermon in the Deer Park at Sarnath.

Candidates for ordination will already be *semaneras* (novices). The ceremony will take place within a *sima* (a specially defined area). An *upajjhaya* (preceptor) must officiate. He will be a senior monk, head of an order or senior incumbent of a monastery, invested with this responsibility. The candidates must be able to recite the *Patimokkha* (rules of discipline). Before the ceremony, new robes will have been made for the candidates, dyed brown or saffron. After it, they will be bound by the 227 rules of the monastic community and the Ten Precepts. In the Mahayana tradition the conventions and ceremonies vary, but the commitment is essentially the same. The robes worn are black in the Zen tradition and maroon in the Tibetan.

Celibacy

The *Vinaya* (Code of Discipline) orders monastic life, which demands celibacy. It is worth noting, however, that in certain Korean and Tibetan orders it is possible for monks and nuns to marry, and that this is the norm for Japanese monks. The Triratna Buddhist Order does not, strictly speaking, have monks and nuns. They may be married with families or be single. However, celibacy is practised by some Order members. Those with families may still choose to live in single-sex communities.

Weddings and marriage

Marriage is regarded in Buddhism as a social and civil matter. Monks therefore do not officiate at weddings, nor are they allowed to be present at the ceremony. Monks will bless a marriage as a separate event, after the ceremony, but the distinction between this and the ceremony itself is quite clear. As one Theravada Buddhist puts it:

> *It's not according to the Vinaya, which is the code of conduct for the monks. They are excluded from taking part in these ceremonies, because the Buddhist monk is a person who has renounced worldly life. He is working on his own salvation, and he is in a monastery which has been provided.*

(John Bowker, *Worlds of Faith*, BBC, 1983, p 207)

Family life

Because Buddhism is traditionally centred upon monastic life and the quest for liberation, it might seem that Buddhists would have little to say about married life and bringing up children. However, more than 95 per cent of Buddhists are lay people, with these issues very much at the centre of their lives.

Sangha has a larger meaning than just 'monastic community'. Indeed, had the Buddha not spread his message to lay people, the tradition would not have developed in the way that it has. The importance of the interdependent relationship between monastic and lay society was always emphasized by the Buddha, and with good reason, as, given the doctrine of rebirth, our station changes in successive lives and the merit accrued by good karma in one life is the only means to elevation in the next. Thus the significance of how one lives life as a lay person, and the way in which children are nurtured are important issues in Buddhist society that have led to the observance of specific rules and customs.

The Buddha said: 'A wise man should avoid unchastity as if it were a pit of burning cinders. One who is not able to live in a state of celibacy should at least not break the purity of another man's wife' (*Suttanipata*, v. 396).

The importance of the family

In the Buddha's Discourses there is much advice to householders on the importance of family life and how it should be conducted. The *Rukkhadamma Jataka* compares the strength of family life to the trees of the forest, which are able to withstand the force of the wind, when a solitary tree, however large, cannot (*Jataka*, Vol. 1, v. 329).

The metaphor is apt for the significance of both family life and sangha generally, suggesting that family ties and spiritual friendship encourage growth in the dharma and resistance to samsaric conditions. The *Sigalovada Suttanta* gives the most specific advice on lay society and family life. Sigola was a young man who showed no interest in the dharma, but who was entreated by his dying father to worship the six quarters of the earth and sky. Ignorant of the meaning of this, he was met one morning by the Buddha taking this advice literally, worshipping in every direction. The Buddha explained the six quarters to him as parents, teachers, wife and children, friends and associates, employees, religious teachers and priests. In each of these relationships, certain duties pertain.

Parents and children

In the relationship between parent and child, the child should:
* *support his or her parents*
* *perform their duties for them*
* *keep up the family and family traditions*
* *be worthy of his or her heritage*
* *offer alms in honour of departed relatives.*

The parent should:
* *restrain the children from evil*
* *direct them toward the good*
* *attend to their education*
* *see them married at a proper age*
* *hand over their inheritance.*

(Digha Nikaya, Vol. III, 180, quoted in H. Saddhatissa, *Buddhist Ethics*,
Wisdom Publications, 1987, p 118)

Husband and wife

In the relationship between husband and wife, the husband should:
* *be courteous to his wife*
* *respect her*
* *be faithful*
* *hand over authority to her*
* *provide her with clothes and adornments.*

The wife should:
* *perform her household duties well*
* *be hospitable to relatives*
* *be faithful*
* *protect the family income*
* *be skilled and industrious in her duties.*

(Digha Nikaya, Vol. III, 190, quoted in H. Saddhatissa, *Buddhist Ethics*,
Wisdom Publications, 1987, p 120)

Birth and upbringing

Traditionally, before her baby's birth, a mother-to-be may visit a temple to receive blessings from the monks. Soon after the birth, too, babies are taken to the temple to receive blessings. Many Buddhists give their children names that begin with auspicious sounds, and a monk may be consulted as to suitable names. Some Western families may wish to give Asian names to their children. Later on in their lives, boys in Burma and Thailand may take temporary ordination as part of their education. This will last for only a matter of weeks in most cases. This rite of passage is unavailable at present to Buddhists in Western countries.

Death and dying

Death and dying are of particular significance in the Buddhist world view, because they are part of the cycle of rebirth, and therefore directly connected to birth itself (rather than being at the other end of life's events). It is important to die well, but also to live every moment as if it were one's last. This is not a morbid outlook. As one Tibetan teacher has said, 'Death is a great adventure.' Of course, fear of death *does* induce morbidity, and Buddhism addresses this issue. All is impermanent in the samsaric realm, and we must accept that. Rebirth is a consequence of this impermanence. Death is the event in the chain of cause and effect that induces rebirth. Sogyal Rimpoche, a Tibetan Lama who has written on the subject of death and dying, examines the issue thus:

> *At the moment of death our life becomes clear. Death is our greatest teacher. But, unfortunately, people in the West think of death only when they are dying. That is a little bit late.*

He also makes the point that:

> *Life is nothing but changes, which are little deaths.*
> (Interview in the *Observer*, 22 November 1992, p 55)

This points to the need to accept and learn from the inevitable results of our karma, of which impermanence and dying are a part.

Funeral rites

When a person is dying it is usual for a monk or lay person to recite appropriate scriptures to them, to remind them of the Buddha's teaching and to calm their mind. In Tibetan Buddhism, *The Tibetan Book of the Dead* is often read to prepare the dying person for the journey through the bardo state, from this life to the next, with the hope that it will result in either liberation or a meritorious rebirth. It is important for the dying person to know that the state of mind in which they die will influence their rebirth.

At funerals, monks conduct the services, giving a talk and chanting scriptures on the theme of impermanence and the transitory nature of life. The ceremony does not dwell on bereavement, but on the qualities of the dead person. In the Soto Zen tradition, the funeral is an ordination ceremony, in which the dead person's faith can be strengthened to help him or her face the Eternal Buddha without fear.

The usual way of disposing of the body is by cremation. When great teachers die, it is usual to preserve their relics in the same way as the Buddha's, and to distribute them to monasteries or centres set up by that teacher, where a *stupa* will be built to house them. These may then become centres of pilgrimage and be regarded as holy shrines.

In conclusion

In this chapter we have surveyed ways in which Buddhism has traditionally fitted into and influenced the social order in different Buddhist countries and examined the associated teachings and practices.

Buddhism has integrated itself into a number of traditional Asian societies and the monastic – lay structure of Buddhism has been influential in the construction of social roles and values. Buddhist beliefs and teachings have been instrumental in determining specific social practices in relation to birth, upbringing, rites of passage and death rituals. Buddhist understandings of karma, rebirth and social responsibility have had a shaping effect on the social order.

9

festivals and ceremonies

This chapter presents the different festivals and ceremonies that Buddhists celebrate. These vary according to the branch of Buddhism and its location, according to whether it was established in South-East Asia, Tibet, China and Japan, or in the West. The flavour and ways of celebrating vary according to local custom. However, most festivals celebrate important events in the Buddha's life, national events associated with Buddhism or important Buddhist figures. Some festivals and ceremonies are more focused on the monastic community but others are influenced by more local customs, such as the veneration of ancestors in Japan. You will learn that, more than any other expression of Buddhism, festivals and ceremonies reflect the diversity of the tradition across different cultures and illustrate the flexibility of Buddhism as it has spread through these cultures. At the same time, they reveal the adaptation and change that has taken place.

There is great diversity in the range of Buddhist festivals and ceremonies because Buddhism has spread into a number of very different cultures in the course of its history. According to the type of Buddhism represented, these festivals tend to focus on the Buddha Sakyamuni, the significant events in his life, his teachings and the Buddhist community, or range wider by including saints, bodhisattvas and other Buddhas and beliefs. What also differs is the way in which these events are celebrated, for each culture brings to them its own particular style and form and a specific calendar year. For these reasons, it is best to divide Buddhist festivals into four main groups, representing the Theravada tradition, the Tibetan tradition, the Chinese-Japanese tradition and the Triratna Buddhist Order.

All Buddhist religious festivals follow the lunar calendar, and most of the important ones are celebrated on full-moon days. Knowing exactly when a particular festival will occur is not such an easy task. The solar calendar varies year by year, so just like Easter in the Christian tradition, Buddhist festival days fall on moveable dates. Buddhists rely on printed calendars for their information, and the festival celebration itself will occur on the appropriate full-moon day (or sometimes on the weekend closest to it in non-Buddhist countries).

Theravada festivals

Wesak

Wesak celebrates the Buddha's birth, enlightenment and death, which are all, according to Buddhist tradition, supposed to have occurred on the same day of the year; as such, this is the most important Theravadin festival. It takes place on the full-moon day of the second month in the Indian year, which, in the Western calendar, occurs in late May or early June. The Indian name for this month is Vaishakha, which, translated into Sinhalese, becomes Wesak, and in Thai, Visakha. Thus the festival is named after the month. Emphasis is placed on the enlightenment of the Buddha, which is the pre-eminent event, as it marks the point at which the dharma was rediscovered by the historical Buddha Sakyamuni. It is customary to put up decorations in local temples and to light lamps after dark, symbolizing enlightenment coming into the world.

Asala

Asala, normally in July, marks the beginning of the Rains Retreat (called *Vas* in Sinhalese) and recalls the preaching of the Buddha's first sermon, the Turning of the Wheel of the Law. As this marks the beginning of the Buddha's ministry, monks preach sermons recalling the event. In the latter half of the month, Sri Lankans stage the Asola Perahara, a spectacular procession in which the relic of the Buddha's tooth is processed through the streets of Kandy. Relics of the Buddha, or of great Buddhist teachers, are usually to be found wherever Buddhist missionary activity has founded new centres. But the history of this event is primarily nationalistic rather than religious.

Kathina ceremony

Held in October or November of the Western calendar, Kathina is organized by lay people in order to present monks with new robes. One robe is ceremonially presented as the Kathina robe to the head of the monastery, to be given to the monk who is, at least in theory, to be the most virtuous. He will be chosen by the abbot.

The robe is made, according to ceremonial prescription, by sewing patches together in such a way as is said to imitate the patchwork of the paddy fields familiar to the early monks on their travels. The community first presents the cloth for the robe, which is marked, cut out and sewn by the monks on the same day, before being given back to the laity for presentation. Another meaning given to the word 'kathina' is 'difficult', which suggests the arduousness of the vocation of a disciple of the Buddha, and the tenacity required to follow the dhamma.

Tibetan festivals

Tibet provides a distinctive culture for Buddhist life, and the terms 'Tibetan' and 'Buddhist' are synonymous within the Tibetan world. Before the invasion of Tibet by China in 1959, little was known of this way of life, but since then, Tibetan Buddhism has established itself in India and across Europe and the United States, with the diaspora led by the present, fourteenth, Dalai Lama and a number of important Buddhist teachers, or lamas, around whom communities have grown. The centre of 'Tibet in exile' is the small town of McLeod Gange, above Dharamsala in the Indian foothills of the Himalayas, where the Dalai Lama has his palace.

The Tibetan calendar is lunar and divided into 12 months; to keep in step with the solar year, it is necessary to add a month during certain years. To keep in phase with the moon, some months are less than 30 days. Some Tibetan festivals commemorate the usual events related to the Buddha's life; others have a peculiarly Tibetan significance.

Losar

Losar is Tibetan New Year, which falls in February. Lasting for 15 days, it commemorates the Buddha's early life, through to his enlightenment and his efforts to establish the dharma during his teaching career. Within Tibet, monks sat their examinations for higher degrees on the fourth day, called the Great Prayer (*Monlam Cheamo*). The fifteenth day is the full-moon day, *Chonga Chopa*, when Tibetan culture comes into its own with the remarkable butter sculptures for which it is famous. These are usually of scenes in the Buddha's life, coloured with different dyes. Tibetans also put on puppet shows on the same themes. Traditionally, the monks of two famous monasteries called the Upper Tantric School (*Gyuto*) and Lower Tantric School (*Gyume*) are responsible for these displays. They are now located in India, and the celebrations take place in Dharamsala.

Saga Dawa

This festival, held on the fifteenth day of the fourth month (the full moon of May in the Gregorian or Western calendar), recognizes the Buddha's birth, enlightenment and death (the equivalent of Wesak). This is the strictest observance day in the Tibetan calendar, when no meat is eaten and lamps are lit everywhere. Circumambulation is another feature of this festival; devotion is shown by going round Buddhist monuments in a clockwise direction, by means of prostration – measuring out the distance with the body and standing where the head faced the ground in a continuously repeated process. Devout Buddhists will also take a vow to fast and be silent for seven days, which symbolizes both the significance of abstinence in Buddhist practice and the Buddha's passing.

Chokhor

This festival commemorates the Buddha's first sermon, the Turning of the Wheel of the Law. Occurring in June or July, on the fourth day of the sixth month, it is a summer festival, associated in the Tibetan climate with fine weather and colourful celebration. The community would carry *xylographs*, scriptures engraved on long, rectangular wooden blocks, and statues, in great processions with a carnival atmosphere. This signified the spread of the dharma through the Buddha's teaching.

Japanese and Chinese festivals

Buddhist influence has waned in China since its peak 1,000 years ago, when it combined with Taoist and Confucian indigenous tradition. In recent history, the Maoist revolution and China's present communist government have repressed Buddhist practice, but not eradicated it. It still survives, particularly in the provinces close to Tibet. Though the Western calendar is influential today, the Chinese still use lunar months, which operate in a similar way to the Tibetan system. Chinese tradition is especially concerned with the remembrance of dead ancestors and the celebration of birthdays, and this influences their Buddhist festivals.

Japan received Buddhism via China, so it is not surprising to find similarities, though variations of Buddhism in Japan have flourished in connection with Shinto, the earlier Japanese religion (which bears similarity with Confucianism in its respect for ancestors, and filial and state order are of great importance). The two main festivals in both countries share common themes. The names referred to here are the Japanese versions.

Gautama Buddha's birth

This is known as *Hana Matsuri* in Japan, where the Buddha's enlightenment and death are remembered separately. It occurs on 8 April, and, correspondingly in the Chinese calendar, on the eighth day of the fourth month. The themes of flowers and water are prevalent, reflecting the mythology of the Buddha's birth itself.

The festival coincides with the flowering of the cherry blossom in Japan, and stalls selling food and gifts are set up in temple courtyards. Folk dancing and acrobatics form part of the celebrations.

The festival of the hungry ghosts

This festival honours dead ancestors. According to Buddhist cosmology, samsara is divided into realms, through which living beings pass. The realm of the hungry ghosts is one of these. In effect it parallels All Soul's Day, but with special significance due to the importance of ancestors in Japanese and Chinese tradition. Occurring in July, or the seventh month in the Chinese calendar (July or August), it lasts for three and seven days, in Japan and China respectively. It recalls the story of Maudgalyayana, or Mu-lien, one of the Buddha's chief disciples who had special powers, through which he was able to visit other realms. On one of his journeys, he found his mother in one of the hells. In some versions she is described as one of the hungry ghosts, who typically suffer from distended stomachs and tiny mouths (illustrating their incapacity to satisfy their desires). The story recounts that he saved her by offering a feast to all buddhas and monks, and by virtue of this act of merit she was raised out of hell by the Buddha using a rope.

Western Buddhist festivals

The Triratna Buddhist Community celebrates the Buddhist year with three main festivals: Buddha Day, Dharma Day and Sangha Day, representing the Three Jewels.

Buddha Day is held on the full moon in May, and celebrates the Buddha's enlightenment. Dharma Day is in July, and Sangha Day in November, according with Kathina. These are times for the Triratna Buddhist Order to come together with friends or *mitras*; interested Westerners are also welcome. The gatherings take place in Triratna Buddhist Community centres, which are usually large houses or halls converted to Buddhist purposes. Ceremonies take place in a shrine room, decorated for the occasion, and include a talk from a senior Order member, a puja with chanting and meditation, and the sharing of food. Sometimes, special events are held for children. Mitra ceremonies are often held after the puja on Dharma Day, when new members of the community, wishing to affirm their commitment do so by taking the Three Jewels, and offer flowers, candles and incense in front of the shrine. On Sangha Day, mitras make these same three offerings as a re-affirmation of their commitment.

In conclusion

In this chapter we have noted how festivals in Buddhist countries and those influenced by Buddhism take on diverse cultural expressions and are linked with differing beliefs, practices and histories. We can conclude the following:

Diversity is an accepted part of the history of Buddhism as it has spread into new cultures. Festivals are expressions of the cultural importance of Buddhism in those societies where it has been influential.

10

Buddhism today: East and West

This chapter considers the way Buddhism has spread from East to West and the ways in which it has adapted to change in the contemporary world. You will learn how Buddhism has survived in India mainly through its attraction for the *dalits* (or untouchables) within the Indian caste system, how it has been influenced in South-East Asia by contact with western society, how Tibetan Buddhism has been promoted in the West following the Chinese occupation of the country and the exile of the Dalai Lama, and how Buddhism in the West has resulted in both a revitalization of traditional practice and innovation. In the West converts to Buddhism, and others attracted to it, have been driven by their interest in meditation and self-development rather than wishing to support a traditional monastic sangha. More eclectic forms of Buddhism have also emerged. Nevertheless, more traditional forms have survived and flourished.

Buddhism in India

Today the Buddhist tradition survives in India, largely through the conversion movement of Dr Bim Ambedka among the *dalits* or untouchables (or, as Gandhi named them, *harijans* – Children of God), which has expanded since its inception in 1956 to at least 3.5 million.

Buddhism in South-East Asia

In the main, Buddhism in South-East Asia is Theravadin. The most significant effect on South-East Asian Buddhism has been the impact of Western society and values in the twentieth century and now in the twenty-first century. Modern influences have stressed the need for Buddhist teachings to be seen as scientific, and adaptable to worldwide social conditions. In major urban centres its 'religiosity', and its adaptation over the course of its history to folklore and local belief, has been played down in order to make it acceptable to Western ways of thinking.

There has also been a rebirth of religious vitality among lay people. In Thailand in particular, a programme of dhamma education has increased significantly in modern times. Equally, meditation-orientated sanghas in Burma and Thailand have sought to revive lay practice. Since the Second World War, over 200 meditation centres have been established in Burma. During the 1960s and 1970s, this revival spread to Thailand and was reinforced by teachers establishing monasteries, where disciplined meditation practice is seen as reviving the vitality of the monastic sangha. One example of this is the Forest Retreat Order of Ajahn Chah, which is now established in the West.

Tibetan Buddhism

The single most dramatic historical event to have an effect on Buddhism in the twentieth century was the Chinese invasion of Tibet, and the subsequent exile of the Dalai Lama in India since 1959.

The key figure in this adaptation is the Dalai Lama himself. His residence is situated in the small town of McLeod Ganj near Dharamsala, in the Himalayan foothills of India, which hosts the largest number of Tibetans in exile within one place. This is regarded as the centre of Tibetan Buddhism while exile continues. However, he also travels the world, balancing the twin needs of sustaining the fabric of Tibetan life in exile and acting as ambassador for its cause and promoting world peace. At the same time, he remains a Buddhist monk.

Buddhism in the West

Buddhism in the West has emerged, partly through immigrant communities arriving in Europe and North America but also through Westerners discovering Buddhism or becoming Buddhist monks in Asia and returning to the West as part of Buddhist missionary activity in the twentieth and twenty-first centuries.

Many different branches of Buddhism have been established, originating in such countries as Thailand, Tibet and Japan. As a result, Britain today has a great variety of Buddhist groups and communities – far more than would be found in any one 'traditionally Buddhist' country. The *Directory of Buddhist Groups*, produced by the Buddhist Society, reported 74 groups in 1979; eight years later there were 191, and this number has continued to grow.

The Triratna Buddhist Community (formerly the Friends of the Western Buddhist Order) deserves its own separate entry here, due to its more radical and controversial interpretation of how Buddhism needs to be adapted to the modern world.

The Triratna Buddhist Community believes that the Buddha's message should be presented in a positive way, such that it is seen as enhancing the society it is in, rather than being separate from it. They emphasize the positive counterpart of each precept. So, for example, the first precept, 'I undertake to refrain from harming living beings', is balanced by 'With deeds of loving kindness I purify my body'. In concert with this, it welcomes Western literature (such as the work of Goethe and William Blake) that represents teachings seen as supporting the Buddhist vision. It accentuates qualities such as good communication, creativity and active involvement in society as ways in which the aim of spiritual evolution can be achieved.

In the United States, Buddhist influence has been felt more keenly in certain areas than in other Western countries. This is partly due to its proximity to Asia on the west coast. At the end of the nineteenth century, Japanese and Chinese families settled in California; the Japanese also settled in Hawaii during the twentieth century after the enforcement of strict immigration laws in California in 1902. Hawaii also became the focus of Buddhist missionary activity in the United States, which in turn led to temples and meditation centres being established on the mainland. In the process of this transference from their original cultural setting, Buddhists have adapted their organizations and forms of service. Buddhist influence has also spread into American cultural life, beyond classically Buddhist institutions, through its attraction as a spiritual philosophy, and a meditative practice.

In conclusion

We may say that the twentieth century was a time of upheaval and progressive change for Buddhism, as its traditional centres were subjected to different political and economic influences. Its missionary activity has increased, but it is too early to say whether this will ultimately have any significant effect.